# CONCILIUM
*Religion in the Seventies*

# CONCILIUM

*Concilium* March, 1977: Dogma

# A PERSONAL GOD?

Edited by
## Edward Schillebeeckx and
## Bas van Iersel

A CROSSROAD BOOK
The Seabury Press • New York

1977
The Seabury Press
815 Second Avenue
New York, N.Y. 10017

Library of Congress Catalog Card Number: 77-80555
ISBN: 0-8164-0361-9
ISBN: 0-8164-2149-8 (pbk.)
Printed in the United States of America

# CONTENTS

# Part III
## Recent Theological Reflection

# Part IV
## The Religious and Political Relevance of God
## as a Personal Being

# Part V
## Bulletin

# Editorial

IN recent years there have been many critiques of theism and the personalist concept of God. Some commentators have even spoken of 'the death of God'. But since then a new sensitivity to the mystical dimension of human life has been evident. This issue of *Concilium* is not devoted to studies of the socio-political suasions behind this religious renewal, however valuable such analyses might be. The revived interest in spirituality was at first directed to oriental experience but recently, above all in North America and then in Europe, there has been a displacement of attention to mystics of the Christian tradition. St John of the Cross has found his old pre-eminence. Many people are engaged in the quest for a more profound dimension of being. The word 'God' is again current in this regard, even though it is not obvious that the religious experiences in question are oriented to the old model of theism. The God at issue is one who transcends the categories of the 'personal divine' and the 'impersonal divine'. That is precisely the complex of problems that we try to examine theologically in this number.

The belief in harmony, in oneness, has been so strong in Asian spirituality, that it offers an implicit critique of the western emphasis on the subjective. In the West, as a consequence of the philosophy of subjectivity, a somewhat different notion of God developed as a condition for the possibility of the human subject. We have to ask whether the Christian mystical tradition does not show that God himself transcends the dilemma of the 'personal' and the 'impersonal' divine. Is God 'a' person? Is he personal?

In the first, philosophical article, Falk Wagner shows to what extent it is possible to attain to a satisfactory concept of person outside a religious context. The bourgeois notion of person—person means self-determining self-consciousness—leads to insoluble theoretical difficulties. Christian ideas of the person have been influenced by the bourgeois notion, so that God has been conceived as absolute self-determination; but an appropriate notion of person is possible only under the inspiration of the dogma of the Trinity. The person is himself in that which is other than himself. An analysis of the conventional theological theistic notion of God and of ideas of the possibility of God-experience is needed. Herbert Vorgrimler in his article draws certain conclusions regarding the nature of our talk about God, especially in prayer. Peter Nemeshegyi examines the differences between a prophetic and a mystical experience of the divine. The two are not incompatible, but point to the danger of exclusivity in this respect. We tend also to talk with a certain readiness of the 'Jewish-Christian tradition': as a contribution to a more exact understanding of Jewish religious and ethical belief in God, Manfred Vogel shows the primary importance of a personal God, or Thou-God, as normative in Jewish tradition and practice. In the Christian tradition, above all in the history of dogma, the notion of 'person' evolved as a theological concept. Raniero Cantalamessa examines the idea of person as it developed from the personalism of the dogma of the Trinity ('personality' and 'impersonality' again). He notes that the concepts 'nature' and 'person' are invalid apart from that dogma, and that they express what believers designate with the term 'triune God'. Though God is inexpressible and has many names, none of which is wholly apposite, Mystery calls out for a name. However great and all-embracing the divine Mystery is, without personal names we are reduced to dumb anonymity (Jan Peters). In a thematic theological article, Piet Schoonenberg asks whether we are bound to regard the living God as personal. Schoonenberg demonstrates the difficulties that arise if we try to talk of God as a person, when he cannot be thought of as 'over there'; yet the border-line between God and man is on man's side, for it is not laid down by God. A dialogue with eastern God-notions is possible on this basis and has positive aspects. Frans Maas studies the dilemma of the 'personal' and 'impersonal' God in Meister Eckhart (as a representative of 'natural mysticism') and St John of the Cross (standing for 'bridal mysticism'). He concludes that both varieties of mysticism elicit the 'personal divine', though by different routes. God himself transcends the 'personal-impersonal' debate. But what is the socio-political tenor, if any, of this complex of problems? Georg Wildmann suggests the political relevance of the Christological and trinitarian notions of person in the history of western society. 'Person' is a concept that cannot be functionalized. George Maloney shows how prayer reveals essential aspects of the problem of the personal divine. The final contribution (Robert B. Mellert) is a detailed article on the largely Anglo-American phenomenon of process theology which is deeply concerned with the topic under discussion here.

We are sure that this *Concilium* makes a serious contribution to the study of a very relevant set of problems in the religious life.

Edward Schillebeeckx
Bas van Iersel

# PART I

*Present Questions*

Falk Wagner

# Self-determination and Person: Man's Inability to Enunciate 'the Personal' adequately outside a Religious Context

## FAILURE OF THE HUMAN PERSONALITY

NOWADAYS anyone who wishes to discuss the human being as a person is confronted by almost insurmountable problems. What has distinguished man up to now and especially in the modern era—his being an individual person, his subjectivity and his personality—seems today to have been dissipated. The bankruptcy of the human personality is the topic appropriate to the age: 'Man as an individual is that which is absolutely replaceable . . . nothing at all'.[1] The personality has become 'its own *persona*'.[2]

The individual of this 'end of the individual' is not the individual 'pure and simple', but a specific individual. This is the individual who in modern philosophy and theology, and in the literary and social context of bourgeois society, was established, maintained and celebrated as a spiritually autonomous personality, or as self-conscious subjectivity.

The fact that man conceives himself as a self-determinative person and has accordingly to posit his autonomy in the competitive struggle of bourgeois society is a view of the human person that seems necessarily to become obsolete as a result of the experience of the modern era. The notion of the person that has developed in modern thought sees the person as based on the concepts of self-determinative or self-definitive self-consciousness and spontaneous (autonomous) subjectivity.

Person, self-consciousness and subjectivity as well as subject may be thought of as more or less synonymous terms inasmuch as self-consciousness and subjectivity refer to the innermost essence of a person. Of course we can define 'person' more precisely by using the terms 'self-consciousness' and 'subjectivity' to characterize the general principle of the person. This principle may be defined as the expression of self-determination and autonomy in regard to nature and history (tradition), and also as the idea of the personality to which the person is 'subject as belonging to the world of the senses'.[3] Personality and person are in this understanding principle and *principiatum*, idea and reality, or general and particular. The idea of personality properly resides in the person insofar as the person is consciously subject to the principle of self-determination. Consequently the human individual is not personality but possesses personality on condition that in his thought and action he is subject to the principle of self-determination and thus exists as a person independent of the influences of nature and history.

### PERSONALITY AND PERSON

The distinction between personality and person corresponds to the basic distinction between determination and the determinable, between reason and the empirical world. It has very significant consequences for the construction of the actual and determined self-consciousness as the logico-categorial core of the human person. That can be seen from Fichte's philosophy. Fichte tries to ground self-consciousness as the absolute ego. The ego is said to produce itself originally and spontaneously as self-postulate, as action, and therefore as a unity of activity and passivity. But this self-postulating *I* has not thereby constituted itself as a real and specifically self-knowing self-consciousness. For the *I* first attains to itself as a self-knowing self-consciousness when in confrontation with the other—with, therefore, the *not-I* or object. The *I* is determined by the object in its very determination of that same object. In this restriction of its activity by the object the *I* becomes conscious of itself. In that action, however, lies the foundation of the fact that the *I*, as a really self-knowing *I*, is *eo ipso* a finite self-consciousness. The idea of the real self-consciousness can only be conceived as finite self-consciousness on the basis of the mediate nature of the activity of the *I* through the reciprocal action of the object. Insofar as the notion of the person is based on that self-consciousness, then the person cannot be conceived in any other way than as finite.

The finiteness of the real self-consciousness and that of the person comprise the logico-conceptual presupposition of Fichte's criticism and rejection of the notion of the personality of God as inappropriate to the definition of God.[4] This criticism subsequently decided philosophical and theological thinking until now, so that every new attempt to conceive of God in a personal sense is mediated through direct or indirect confrontation with the arguments developed by Fichte.

## BOURGEOIS PERSONALITY

There was also a recurrent emphasis in nineteenth-century thought on the expression of God's absoluteness together with that of his spiritual personality. This interest in the conceivability of God as a personality derives primarily from the interest of man in the autonomy of his spiritual-moral personality. As Goethe makes one of his lovers say: 'The greatest happiness of humankind is personality'. That is no more than a literary expression of the key notion of the bourgeois age. The interest of the bourgeois subject in his direct self-determination issues in the notion of personality, which no one now has. Since, however, the self-determination of the personality constantly meets with setbacks under the influence of nature and society, the human subject seeks in God that personality which determines itself wholly of itself, and which therefore is withdrawn from any form of determination by anything or anyone else. Because God is taken as representing *the* successful instance of self-determining personality, man—even under the conditions of a spirit restricted by nature and society—can retain the idea of realizing himself as a moral-religious personality. The similarly and wholly religio-theological motives which led to the conception (in spite of Fichte's critique) of the personality as compatible with God's absoluteness, are therefore mediated by the interest of the bourgeois subject in being able to retain his own self-determination as expressed in the principle of personality.

It is precisely this attempt of the bourgeois subject to conceive himself as personality, subjectivity, or self-determining self-consciousness, which present-day conditions have invalidated. This invalidation is indicated in the notion of the 'end of the individual'.[5] This implies that the *principium individuationis* in which the modern bourgeois subjectivity is grounded and which is identical with the principle of self-preservation and self-determination, is to be made responsible for the collapse of the individual as an autonomous person.

If the individual subject is to be constituted in the sense of the principle of self-determination, he is required to master and control inner and outer nature. For the sake of his self-determination, the individual has *both* to liberate himself from his natural needs, inclinations and drives, *and* to become independent of the effects of external nature. In the course, however, of the realization of the principle of self-determination through human subjects, the dominative component of self-determination recoils on those very subjects. That is primarily obvious in the nature of competition, which holds sway in all sectors of bourgeois society. The principle of self-determination is no longer directed solely against inner and outer nature but against competing individuals. For what is apparent in the competitive struggle of individuals is the principle of self-determination as such, which is ultimately transmitted to the social system and its sub-systems in such a way that the individual as such—in other words, apart from its system-functional rôles—disintegrates. The principle of self-determination succeeds at the expense of the self. That brings the individual person into a state of crisis, which may be said to be created by the self-conscious individual. The individual person who, according to the idea of personality, has insisted on the realization of the principle of self-determination, is dissolved with the generalization and absolutization of that same principle. Since the individual subject has prepared his own desuetude on the basis of the principle he himself has obeyed, he is not unprepared for the criticism which twentieth-century philosophical, social-scientific and theological thought as a whole directs against the *directly* self-determining subjectivity. This critique clearly dispenses with any attempt to conceive the human person, in accordance with the principle of *direct* self-determination, as a wholly autonomous subjectivity. In view of this failure, human existence-as-a-person is obviously closed to objective description. What remains of the autonomous person regresses into an unfathomable inwardness, leisure pursuits and sub-culture.

### APORIA OF THE SELF-DETERMINATIVE SELF-CONSCIOUSNESS

If human being-a-person suffers from the predominance of the principle of direct self-consciousness, that clearly is not due only to the absolutization of self-determination. An aporia may be expected to be inherent in the principle of self-determination which must lead to a form of fulfilment inadequate for the human individual. And in fact an aporia is involved in the concept of self-determinative self-consciousness which undermines the notion of the person. The principle of self-determinative self-consciousness serves as a basis of explanation and foundation for the form which human existence takes. This principle is aporetic inasmuch as it cannot offer any explanation and foundation of itself. The self-determinative and self-postulating self-consciousness must confront itself in the attempt to constitute itself as something unexplained. In the process, the self-explanation of the self-determinative subjectivity is confounded. In order to explain that self-consciousness which was originally to have been explained by sheer self-postulation, the self-consciousness already presupposes itself in its unity of moments: in other words, in both positing and being posited, determining and determined, and subject and object. This aporia of circularity recurs in all attempts to explain subjectivity by the construction of a direct and original subject-object unity. All such attempts depend on the same *petitio principii*: in order to ground the directly self-determinative subject-object unity, that very unity is already presupposed—but without explanation.[6] That applies also to what analytical philosophers treat under the term 'ego' or 'I'. For the pronominal circumlocution of the index term 'I' is also circular if someone formulates it in the first person and says, for instance: 'I use the term "I" to designate myself.' 'By "I" I mean myself.'

The circular aporetic self-explanation of self-determinative self-consciousness is objectified in the major systematic projects of the philosophy of subjectivity inasmuch as there primordially direct self-determination and the subject-object unity can never be validly conceived in the course of their realization. Instead a distinction remains between principle and *principiatum*, between the essence and appearance of subjectivity; this means that instead of a successful realization of self-determination, we have unending progress: approximation or identification with particular objectifications. No absolute-ideal phenomenon accords with the original subject-object unity of self-determinative subjectivity under the conditions of its realization which implies a distinction between subject and object.

Precisely this lasting distinction between unconditioned principle and mere conditioned realization of self-determination occurs in the area of social and political intercourse with self-determination, and occurs in the form of permanent competition between individual and general subjects. The competitive struggle of bourgeois subjects and that of classes, social groups and nations express the fact that the self-determination of individual and general subjects can never be pursued as such, but only in a never-ending process of alien determination. Then the self-determinative self-consciousness experiences itself in the medium of its historical realization as alienated from itself.

To summarize, the failure of the notion of the individual person referred to in the phrase 'end of the individual' is grounded in an aporia of principle: namely, that the self-determinative self-consciousness can attain to an explanation and grounding of itself only by means of a vicious circle. Insofar as the explanation and realization of human being-a-person are also affected by this inconsistent self-explanation of self-consciousness, one might suggest that the notion of person should be distinguished or even separated from that of self-consciousness and that of subjectivity, in order thus to enable the person to escape the context of the deficient, because viciously circular, theory of self-consciousness. Such an attempt is not, however, possible since the modern understanding of being-a-person is very closely bound up with the concepts of self-consciousness and subjectivity. Therefore it is more appropriate to redefine the personal and to try to reconstitute the concept of subjectivity.

## THE CONCEPT OF DIVINE-ABSOLUTE SELF-DETERMINATION

The aporia of the directly self-determining self-consciousness is not alien to the Christian religion. In fact the Christian religion in its reflective form, which is theology, has always responded to this aporia; indeed, we might say that the answer to this aporia was co-incident with the beginning of Christian theology as apparent in the notions of the incarnation, death and resurrection of God, in what is basically a conceptual form. For what do those terms mean in regard not to their soteriological aspect but to the nature of God himself? This question can only be answered adequately if we start from a conceptual and structural explication of the idea of God, and do not shrink from straining the idea somewhat. Only by a reflective-notional explanation can we successfully reground the concept of person as it may be derived from reflective Christian theology. Christian theology can only solve the aporia of the person concept by transcending the conceptual level of that very aporia.[7]

God may be conceived as creator, all-determining reality, almighty subject, or whatever. These conceptions depend essentially on terms such as *aseitas, actus purissimus* and *causa sui*. These enact a sublation to the absolute self-determination of the divine nature. God determines himself of and by himself. He is what he is because he is. However, no one in the history of thought has ever succeeded in conceiving the notion of divine-absolute self-determination consistently and without any aporia. For if the distinction between determining and being determined, activity and passivity, or—figuratively—creator and creation, is consequent on divine determination as self-determination, then this distinction implies a presupposition which is incompatible with absolute self-determination. It consists in the fact that an autonomy which is relative in regard to the moment of active determination inheres in the moment of being determined: of, that is, passivity. The self-determinative power of God presupposes for itself with the moment of passive being determinedness, of powerlessness, a presupposition relative to which power can first declare itself as power. This presupposition has to be made *for* the divine postulation and determination. But that raises the question whether the presupposition in question is adequate to divine determination; to, that is, that moment for which the presupposition was presupposed. The question of the correspondence of the postulation of power and presupposed powerlessness shows that divine power must necessarily presuppose the relative autonomy of passive determinedness, so that this presupposition can accord with what it was presupposed for: namely, divine self-determination. But that introduces a process in the course of which the distinction between determining and being determined, between power and powerlessness, disappears, is resolved. For inasmuch as the presupposed powerlessness of self-determinative power becomes adequate for the sake of that power, the distinction between power and powerlessness is cancelled. The distinction between determining and being determined is dissolved by the indifference of the elements distinguished. Determining and being determined, or divine power and human powerlessness, are in equilibrium, because presupposed powerlessness in its relative autonomy corresponds to the determinative power of which it is a presupposition. That divine power and human powerlessness, active determination and passive being determined, 'cancel out', indicates first of all that God, insofar as he is conceived as absolute self-determination, is not that God.

## BEGINNING OF CHRISTIAN THEOLOGY

This disappearance of God as absolute Lord is not so to speak the end, but the beginning of Christian theology. For if we ask what the concepts of incarnation and death of God mean in terms of God's nature itself, they mean: God takes the place of man, of passive determinedness, and man exchanges his place with God, by killing the God-become-man who fails on account of his presupposition. The incarnation and death of God means the dissolution of the distinction between God and man, and at the same time of that between absolute self-determination and passive alien-determination. Hence it is clear that Christian theology can never make the notion of directly self-determining subjectivity the essential or inclusive concept for understanding the person. Conceptually interpreted, theology shows that the 'absolute instance' of direct self-determination (in other words, divine self-determination) fails on account of its immanent aporia: the presupposed presupposition. Christian theology shows why subjectivity and being-a-person—if conceived in accordance with the structure of direct self-determination and autonomy—are doomed to dissolution.

Theology can explain the reason for the modern debate about the 'end of the individual'. The autonomous individual cannot be grounded solely on its own basis. Self-determination presupposes alien determination, autonomy, and heteronomy, on the basis of which presupposition the notion of directly self-determinative being-a-person is shown to be ill-conceived.

## TRINITARIAN NOTION OF GOD

But Christian theology does not end with the failure of divine-absolute self-determination. It begins precisely there, where its passes, on the basis of the indifference of self-determination and other-determination, from God and man to the constitution of the true concept of divine and human subjectivity. The indifference of self- and other-determination can be seen not only as a negative but as an affirmative result. Indifference means then that both change places: active is replaced by passive, and passive by active; so that passivity takes the place of activity, and activity the place of passivity. If this reciprocal substitution is conceived as an *identical* process, in other words *eodem actu*, it is clear that inasmuch as active changes to passive, passive is also manifested as active. Inasmuch as active and passive replace one another as an identical process, passivity occurs in place of activity, and activity in place of passivity; so that in changing places, active and passive are at home. Active and passive therefore explain themselves in that which is other than themselves as themselves. This self-explanation in the other is only adequately conceived if seen as a single identical process indicating that the *self* (active) is at home in the *other* (passive).

This conceptual structure of self-explication in the other is in fact the inclusive or essential concept of Christian theology, for it represents the Christian and trinitarian notion of God. This structure found its actual figurative instance in the Resurrection. In conceptual terms, the resurrection is sublation to the level of the trinitarian notion of God. The trinitarian notion of God is properly conceived only when derived from the failure of the absolute self-determination of God. The affirmatively conceived indifference of self- and other-determination is the structure of the trinitarian God: God (*1*) displays himself in that which is other (*2*) than himself, so that in that other he is also in himself (*3*). The general divine determination therefore applies to itself in such a way that it determines itself in its self-determination as that which is determined (the other), and at the same time in the determination of its being-determined is in itself. The divine self-conception is mediated accordingly by means of self-distinction: that is, God conceives himself in that which is other than himself. In that the divine determination is self-applied, it determines itself as determined determination, distinct from pure determining, but in such a way that the determined distinction is determined as that which is determined, and thus declares itself as identical with the determining. The conceptual-structural constitution of the trinitarian notion of God consists in the fact that God in the determining of himself determines himself as that-which-is-determined, and thus is in himself in the determined as that which is other than the determining. The trinitarian concept of God is therefore the resolution of the aporetic notion of directly absolute self-determination: Divine self-determination is mediated through the determined as that which is other than the determining, but in such a way that the determining is identical with itself in the determining of that which is determined. Therefore God explicates himself in his distinction as himself.

The fact that determining determines its difference can also be expressed thus: Determining as negation negates the determined as negative. The general determining is then negation of any possible determinedness, and any possible negative. But since *everything* can be negated by reason of the general subjection to negation of that which is determined, that is true also of negation or determination itself. Negation applies to itself, and in the negation of itself transforms itself into negated and determined determining. Thereby the *distinction* as such is posited by which general determination is mediated. Conceptually, that means that general divine determination posits distinction as world in the self-negation of its (divine determination's) universal determining. In its conceptual constitution, the world is therefore none other than the distinction which is posited as such. But does that mean a collapse of the unity of determination and being determined, of God and his other, which are comprised in the divine determining, into a difference of universality and particularity, God and world? That is only the case if it can be shown of the posited distinction, of the determined and particular as such, that it is in ítself identical with the universal determining.

The accordance of the particular, of the world, with general determination, God, cannot be demonstrated in that the determining determines that which is determined. For if that which is determined is identical with the general determining, then that identity cannot be explained by recourse to the general determination itself. Instead, it must be shown of that which is determined *as such*, that it accords with the determining. If that which is determined is conceived *as such*, then it is the determined which is determined, or conceived, and the determinedness which is determined. Determinedness as such is non-determining. Therefore determined determinedness as determined = negated non-determining determining itself. The particular posited for itself as the determined which is determined thus declares itself to itself as the self-determining. This self-determining is, as the *subject*, the manifest unity of determining and being determined, of universality and particularity or, figuratively, the manifest unity of God and man.

### THE SON OF GOD

This manifest unity of universality and particularity can also be conceived as the constructive representation of the one *Son of God*. For inasmuch as he posits himself in his particularity in relation to the divine universality in the determinedness of his being-the-Son, he is in himself in determinedness: that is, he is identical with himself and universal. For the determinedness of his being-the-Son is for him, the Son, determined determinedness: that is, a determinedness which is of itself. Therefore the coming of the Son in his determinedness takes place in a boundless universality and particularity. By positing himself in the determinedness of his being-the-Son, the Son makes being-the-Son his own, and therein is in himself and universal.

With being-the-Son as the manifest unity of general and particular, of God and man, Christian theology also conceives the new constitution of the notion of subjectivity and of the person. There is no fixed *I* as substrate to subjectivity. Instead the *I* results before all else from the process of its self-objectification. At first the *I* does not occur as *I* but only in the form of determinatenesses—specific differences—in thoughts, ideas, deeds and feelings. The *I* is not initially 'there', and subsequently thinking or acting. Instead the *I* is primarily present only as the thought 'I': that is, as the *I* determined by thinking, imagining, acting or feeling. This determined *I* can also be known as the 'self'. Accordingly the self aims at an objectified *I*, an *I* objectified in determined thinking and action, not at the *I*-subject, but at the *I*-object or the thought *I*. Only if this determined self conceives itself as objectified self, and selves itself as this determinedness, does the *I* exist as *I*.

It is through determined thoughts and actions that the self is posited to itself. Therefore the self does not appear to itself as the self itself, but as the self determined and objectified through thoughts and actions. The self is therefore determined only as determined self. The self is a determinateness which is determined through that very determinateness: that is, through itself. To be determined through oneself in the determinateness of self and thus to be in oneself, is the *I*. The *I* is therefore neither originally-directly being-in-itself or self-determination, nor is it the self self-posited directly (that is, by means of determined thoughts and actions), but the *I* is the self in itself posited to self in thoughts and actions and therefore identical with itself. The *I* is consequently neither mere abstract identity and universality, as is asserted of *directly* self-determining subjectivity, nor the mere determinateness of the self. Instead the *I* as the manifest unity of universality and particularity is *that-which-determines-self*. As that-which-determines-self, it is distinguished from direct self-determination in that it conceives itself as identical with itself only by way of the self-posited determinateness of the self.

That is the concept of the concrete $I$ as expressed in an exemplary and absolute manner in the one Son of God in Jesus Christ. This concrete $I$ is then also determined as person. Person may be spoken of only insofar as an $I$ is in itself in distinction from itself, in the determined self-posited self. Person is manifest and existent self-distinction of universality and particularity, but in such a way that the person is in himself in the determined self in his own self-distinction.

This concept of the person as a manifest-existent unity of universality and particularity also enables the moments of the immanently trinitarian self-distinction of God to be seen as persons. For only on the basis of the manifest unity of universal and particular is a person capable of finding in another person not a limitation of self but self-fulfilment.

## THE FREEDOM OF THE PERSON

Under the conditions of finite-human personal existence, the person is not in himself in an ultimate and conclusive way in a determinateness of the determined self-posited self, and therefore identical with himself. Instead the human person undergoes a process of development in the course of which he finds his particular fulfilment in a determinateness of the self which can be replaced by other specific differences. It is also true that the human person in any determinateness of himself is in himself and identical with himself. Inasmuch as the person finds fulfilment in a particular determinateness of his self-posited self, he is *free*. The freedom of the person is grounded accordingly in his capacity for development. Just as he is in himself and identical with himself in every determinateness of himself, so he is not ultimately attached to any of these determinatenesses. Rather he can transcend every determinateness of himself on the basis of his being-a-person: that is, on the basis of his manifest-existent unity of universality and particularity; and can thus realize his identity in other determinatenesses of his self-posited self. The human person is therefore still person but at the same time he is not, precisely because he already is person. For if the person had not conceived himself already as a manifest-existent unity of universality and particularity, he would not have found his particular fulfilment in other determinatenesses of his self-given self but would have met with a definitive restriction and dissolution. In this structure of the person as manifest unity of universality and particularity, we find the ground of the fact that competition between individuals can be resolved by communication between persons who are only really (in) themselves in the transcending of their selves. It is true too of the relation of person and society that the person can play a rôle as a person and be a person while playing a rôle only on the basis of its manifest unity of universality and particularity. Hence the concept of a person obtained through concept analysis of the Christian notion of God is also the essential or inclusive concept of true humanity, which is no longer obstructed by the principle of direct self-determination.

*Translated by V. Green*

## Notes

1. M. Horkheimer and T. W. Adorno, *Dialektik der Aufklärung* (Frankfurt am Main, 1969), p. 154.

2. T. W. Adorno, *Stichworte* (Frankfurt am Main, 1969), p. 54.

3. Immanuel Kant, *Kritik der praktischen Vernunft* (Hamburg, 1959), p. 155 (*Critique of Practical Reason*).

4. Cf. F. Wagner, *Der Gedanke der Persönlichkeit Gottes bei Fichte und Hegel* (Gütersloh, 1971), pp. 19–112.

5. Cf. M. Landmann, *Das Ende des Individuums* (Stuttgart, 1971); J. Habermas, *Legitimationsprobleme im Spätkapitalismus* (Frankfurt am Main, 1973), p. 162ff.

6. Cf. D. Henrich, *Fichtes ursprüngliche Einsicht* (Frankfurt am Main, 1966); *id.*, 'Selbstbewusstsein. Kritische Einleitung in eine Theorie', in Hermeneutik und Dialektik, Vol. I (Tübingen, 1970), pp. 257–84; U. Pithast, *Über emige Fragen der Selbstbeziehung* (Frankfurt am Main, 1971); P. Reisinger, 'Reflexion und Ich-Begriff' in *Hegel-Studien*, Vol. 6 (1971), pp. 231–65; F. Wagner, *op. cit.*, pp. 48ff; *id., Schleiermachers Dialektik* (Gutersloh, 1974), pp. 137ff; K. Cramer, 'Erlebnis', in *Hegel Studien*, supp. vol. 11 (1974), pp. 537–603.

7. In the background of the following considerations is the transition from the logic of essence to that of concept in Hegel's *Science of Logic*.

Herbert Vorgrimler

# Recent Critiques
# of Theism

### EXPERIENCES

THE God question in the modern era arose—not exclusively, though
primarily—from three complexes of problems in the area of experience.

1. According to numerous testimonies by would-be believers and
non-believers which we must take seriously, God is no longer experienced, or else he is experienced in the mode of his non-presence. This
non-experience of God is to be distinguished from the terms in which it
is represented: the 'death of God' or the 'loss of direct experience of
God' are significant though almost short-circuit circumlocutions for
the alteration of God-experience from what it meant for Augustine,
Francis of Assisi or Martin Luther.[1]

2. The crimes and disasters of this century have further radicalized
the as yet inadequately answered theodicy problem. It is not obvious
how the 'price of human freedom' paid in terrible suffering is to be
reconciled with a God who is both almighty and loving. Even men
whose outlook is fundamentally religious and pious try to reconcile the
nature and will of God and ask whether the pains and sacrifice will
ever be compensated—in, for instance, a future life of some kind.

3. The more intense experiences of modern men include not only
that of human powerlessness and divine silence, but those in which
mankind tries out new capabilities with success. This experience too
has consequences for the understanding of God. He has become unnec-
essary as a hypothesis for explaining the world, for dealing with catas-
trophes, and for the progressive humanization of mankind, and is therefore clearly 'unusable'. Faith and theology have to take into account

the fact that God no longer occurs in the area of empirical experience, of this-worldly values, and the utilizable.

### CRITIQUE OF THEISM

These three areas of practical experience all over the world contributed to the subjection of theism to an increasingly radical theological critique, at first quite justifiably, since theology has to start from all experiences which mankind has of God. I shall describe some essential elements of the mid-European criticism of theism in the course of this article.

But what exactly is this understanding of God, which has been known as 'theism' since Ralph Cudworth (d. 1688)? It might be summarized as the 'conviction of the existence of an absolute, world-transcendent, personal God, who made the world from nothing and permanently sustains it, who enjoys all those attributes of infinity, almighty power, perfection and so on', about which there was unanimity in Judaism, Christendom and Islam from the Middle Ages onwards.[2] We must add to Cudworth's idea of theism that which produces the theodicy. It is not in the highest cosmic ruler but in the nature of the created that we must look for the distinction between good and evil. Kant thought it important to differentiate between theisms:[3] on the one hand, a conception of God which abstracted from the revelation of God, and wished to ground the existence of God, his nature and his attributes in the capacity of human reason, so that an a priori 'natural theology' was born; and, on the other hand, a theological systematics which tried to synthesize the biblical testimonies to God.

It is obvious that the Protestant theology which based itself on the word of God could never agree to a consensus with aprioristic philosophical theism. In regard to Catholic theology, it is sometimes claimed that Vatican I dogmatized theism.[4] The teachings of Vatican I on God, the creator, and his attributes (Denzinger 3001), his providence (D 3003), and the adequacy of the natural light of human reason for cognition of God (D 3004, 3026) do not, however, imply that a 'natural theology' operating apart from divine revelation was taken as the starting-point of Christian theology and that revelation was only reflected on a posteriori. Vatican I's deliberations follow instead a salvific line, whereby a wholly natural conceivability of God (as the natura pura) is a purely theoretical possibility, and special attention is paid to the cumulative enumeration of divine attributes and recourse to providence. Formulas from the first century are repeated non-analytically. But Vatican I was as little concerned as any other council exhaustively to demonstrate the relation of God to the world and to humanity. It wished only to guard against the tendency to identify God and world or humankind, or so to approximate them to one another that they were virtually indistinguishable. When, therefore, the Church's dogmas—abstracting from the work of Jesus Christ and from the effect of the divine Spirit—speak of God as a person, they talk of his independence and freedom in principle (but not his concrete, factual independence and freedom) in regard to the world and to mankind. It is significant that the Church's magisterium never undertook a fundamental study of the theodicy problem. Hence the narrow limits within which one can talk of theism as binding for Catholic theology.

There was an immense increase in critiques of theism all over the world from 1960 onwards. A primary motive might be seen as a desire to protect God from treatment as an object in faith, religiosity and theology, or from a tendency to reify him, or even—as a consequence of the transcendence model which often accompanies theism—to transcendentalize him. The critique of theism can also be a theological attempt to discover new ways of experiencing God (an attempt which, in view of the evanescence of the experience of God, should have been undertaken by Vatican I and II, but is clearly beyond the capabilities and powers of the magisterium). How is the history of the faith and hope of mankind to be reconciled with the experiences of the modern age? Another strong motive for the critique of theism was a desire to oppose the ideological misuse of theism by certain interested secular and ecclesiastical bodies. A theism which sees God's creativity as something in the prehistoric past, and his providence which now sustains the world, as the legitimization of the *status quo*, too easily contributes to a situation in which the defenders of present ownership (in state theory, property, penal law, and so on) advertise themselves as guardians and proponents of the divine will and thus can further restrict God's function. Supposedly maintaining the substance of faith, they deprive God of the power to guide the world and mankind to his future. In all theological projects in which God is seen as the future of world and mankind, there is an implicit or explicit criticism of conventional theism, which is always open to ideological abuse.

Modern criticism of theism is largely dependent theologically on Paul Tillich and Rudolf Bultmann. Tillich's intended programme was the 'end of theism', which he tried to bring about himself by conceiving 'God above God', by setting the divine, non-anthropomorphic God over the biblical and ecclesiastical God. This 'God over God' is discernible in the theoretically non-derivable and therefore 'absolute faith' of the 'courage to be';[5] an adequate description for this God is 'ground of all being'. Existential thought would allow the retention of the qualitative distinction between God and man, without conceiving God as other worldly; God is 'being itself' or, anthropologically, 'that which unconditionally concerns us'. The attempt to conceive 'being itself' radically led Tillich to negate those attributes of the Existent that were less significant than being itself, and therefore to negate the existence and essence of God. God cannot be understood as the 'highest being', because then he would be characterized as the part of a whole. In this respect, Tillich sharply refuses to describe God as a 'person' or as a 'personal God'. These terms would lead again to the anthropomorphic, other-worldly God of theism, a person alongside other persons. With this rejection of the God-as-a-person concept Tillich enters a tradition in the history of ideas which goes back to the 'atheism quarrel' of 1798–99.[6] According to Tillich, God as the ground of all that is personal cannot be a-personal or sub-personal; and a dialogical relation of man to God, in the sense of the traditional idea of prayer, and a providence guiding the cosmic process are alien to Tillich's thought. Providence means holding to one definite meaning of human history, and the practice of prayer means an actualization of the 'mystery of being' and of that 'which unconditionally concerns us'. Tillich's critics, who examined his thought with special intensity in the late 1960s,[7] doubted the suitability of existentialism for a revision of theism, and that it was possible to reconcile Tillich's with the biblical understanding of God.

Bultmann was more radical than Tillich in his reluctance to make assertions about God's 'being-in-himself', because man as an historical being can have no knowledge of God's being.[8] God, a 'transcendent reality', cannot belong to the world of the existent and at the same time be a being 'above or outside the world'. Transcendent reality is conceivable within the world. It confronts men like a light and makes them aware that 'they are graced as well as summoned in their existence by this transcendent reality'.

Hence the reality of God is at work in the world, in the medium of the human spirit. But it cannot be objectified in thought; and in this sense Bultmann belongs among the Protestant theologians who would reject the objectification and therefore the cancellation of God, and at the same time look for a revised notion of transcendence.[9] Bultmann retains the possibility of speaking, in spite of the theodicy problem, of the almighty power and providence of God: not in the sense of objectifying thought, but only as a testimony of individual faith which acknowledges the Almighty in a desperate 'nevertheless' in regard to the actual circumstances of life, and similarly relies on God's cosmic rule as far as the causally conditioned understanding of the world of the natural and historical sciences is concerned.[10] Divine terminology of theistic origin such as the word 'person' is not (as far as Bultmann is concerned) to be used in such legitimate discourse about an active God.

In the theology that followed Bultmann's viewpoint, the rejection of theism was carried further. Herbert Braun declared that the idea of a 'divinity existing in himself, controlling the course of history', was a barrier to faith. Contrary to the 'static aspect of God-concepts', he wanted to understand God as a 'trans-psychological' event in the area of common humanity. As a New Testament exegete, Braun thought that that allowed a legitimate extension of a process already apparent in Scripture. 'Man and man, man in his common humanity, implies God';[11] but Braun also sees the capacity for love as dependent on something unavailable to men. For Dorothee Sölle, with the palpable end of the interventions and indeed of the presence of God in history, and with the awareness of the moral postulate of the disappearance of the idea of an Almighty, the end has also come for a theism in which an autonomous God is placed 'over there', alien to man.

With this notion of God, the idea of a supernatural and therefore of a prenatal and postmortal existence has disappeared.[12] In Sölle's theology God still has a future. He possesses 'as yet unawakened possibilities', he is in the present but only as *Deus absconditas*, a 'God without qualities'. God is said to occur in human love, and therefore the idea of a personal God set over against man is unreasonable and unhelpful to an understanding of faith. According to Sölle, the God of Jesus is already marked by weakness and dependency: 'Reference to God adds nothing to the Christ project'.[13] For her, the practical theism of those who trust in providence and expect their prayers to be heard comes under suspicion of ideology; it reveals the type of mind that would like to keep existing human impoverishment.

The Swiss theologian Ulrich Hedinger in his sketch of a 'messianic theology'[14] rejects theism under one of its aspects, the notion of perfection. Theism accepts a perfect God-being, who should have a perfect form of reference to men. If one confronts this theism with suffering, it becomes obvious that suffering here can be understood only as a divine pedagogical measure or punishment, redolent of scorn for mankind. In a programme for the 'deperfectionization of God', the God who is really declared dead is the chastizing 'almighty Father' who operates with suffering and the cross. God's nature is instead to be understood as radical love that has always existed and will exist in the future, and that has an advantage over man—one which will be included in the realization of the eschatological community between God and man. In this connexion, 'messianic theology' indicates that the creative being of God and the createdness of man and the world are only promised, still future truth. That everything was 'very good' when created, remains to be realized; the creation is to be 'fulfilled in the fulfilment of the imperative hope of God and man'; in this process of reciprocal reference, God is first and foremost creator, and man is first and foremost man. The God of love attains to his perfection only with the kingdom of God. In view of actual poverty and the theodicy problem, Hedinger sees no other Christian possibility in regard to God than that of petition or lamentation. The difference between the (present) God of love and the God of promised fulfilment is the 'location' of petition and questioning for men who cannot accept present non-redemption.

### TOWARDS AN ENLIGHTENED THEISM

In the discussion of these and related critiques, voices were also raised in defence of a refined theism. At first these were Protestants. According to H. Gollwitzer, there is an irreducible core of theism; in this he agrees wholly with Christian belief in God, in other words, the need for faith to formulate 'theistic propositions': that is, those 'in which God is the grammatical subject of an active proposition.'[15] Gollwitzer doubts whether 'Christian faith can still express itself, if it allows propositions to be prohibited in which God is the subject of an active statement, whether he exists linguistically in such propositions (however much they, like all human pronouncements, are to be protected against misinterpretation).'

H. Ott speaks of a true, existentially illuminative, 'existentiell' and existential depth of theism.[16] Ott also sees the primitive anthropomorphic image of God of a naive theism as justifiably obsolete. But enlightened theism has always realized that 'God is not only "outside" the world but at the same time in the truest sense *in* the world'.[17] Against Pannenberg, and invoking Tillich, Ott considers it legitimate and possible to speak of God as a person, in which case the subject(God)-object(man) is dismissed as inappropriate. The human *I* consists, as Buber said, in its 'thou-assurance'. The thou-experience consists in the fact that the *I* knows that it is addressed. Ott calls this basic experience 'inter-personality' and uses a term from trinitarian theology to categorize it—'perichoresis'. Since the human ego knows that it is transcendentally addressed, e.g., in the question of meaning, the Thou which addresses it here (and then of course in the Gospel) can be called 'person' only in a mere analogous sense. It would be better to call it 'super-person'. As a personal mode of being, 'God's reality is an answer addressed to human-personal reality. As that which is super-personal, it both encloses and transcends the personal acts of man in a way he can no longer understand.[18] Theism cannot be understood as aprioristic natural theology. Instead Jesus' message is to be *interpreted* theistically

—as the word of a God who is ready to talk. A theism understood in this way is, Ott thinks, acceptable to Protestant theologians, because the theistic interpretation already depends on God's grace.[19] Moltmann expressly rejects theism,[20] and for him too the theodicy question takes a political form—with Auschwitz, as for Sölle a key-word—and in this form precisely is now the all-inclusive horizon of the quest for and question about God. But in spite of this crisis in metaphysical theology, he wants to retain the notion of God's being. Earlier, the religious need of men demanded a mystery of highest authority and almighty power, and earlier theology accorded divine being all the characteristics of finite being. But the notion of God thus obtained is irreconcilable with the biblical idea of proclamation from the cross. Christian theology 'has to conceive God's being in suffering and death and ultimately in the death of Jesus, if it is not to give up.'[21] Moltmann is unable to accept the non-suffering, almighty God of crude theism, who is for Moltmann an imperfect being because he is incapable of powerlessness. But assertions about the personal being of God are possible: 'God's being is in suffering, and suffering is in God's very being, because God is love.'[22]

Catholic contributions to the revision of theism also deserve mention. The theology of Karl Rahner does not (as is claimed) start from philosophy but in the experience of God. With the vocabulary of negative theology, Rahner speaks of the experience of darkness, silence and the namelessness of God. He understands these 'dark' experiences as orienting the transcendental dynamism of man to the cross and therefore to the resurrection of Jesus as the place where God is to be discovered as love. The God who has communicated himself to that which is other than himself, and has suffered and died in that other, is experienceable therefore as the love which has given itself in death.[23] Rahner thinks that this God cannot be reached by metaphysics, which attains only to the horizon which is always afar off. For philosophical theism, God always remains the essentially unknown. Therefore metaphysics can neither know God's nature nor make positive deductions about his attributes: the human concept of the absolute remains 'empty'.[24] Theism is accordingly only legitimate to the extent that it is an attempt to reflect on and understand the revelatory self-communication of God. In theism, God is only actualized insofar as he has made himself *the* object for men.

In a special confrontation with Sölle's thought, E. Kunz associates an enlightened theism with personalistic thought.[25] Kunz cannot understand truth and love as projections of man. Between human questioning and action and the self-validating reality of truth and love there is an 'ontological' distinction. Only a source of the claim of absolute commitment, rightly characterized as the 'absolute Thou', could demand absolute commitment and responsibility from man. Justice and peace, according to Kunz, cannot consist in men's acceptance of one another in all their restriction and finiteness. Men can only accept one another because they hope for a fulfilling confrontation, and therefore hope for more than any mere immanent completion of humankind could ensure. According to Kunz, the love emanating from Jesus exceeds human possibilities. Its origin is to be sought in a reality that exists independently of human consciousness and predates man's love. Relations between men are determined in that a man is loved by the absolute source of love before his fellow man turns to him. In this way, on the basis of a reflection on human fundamental human values and achievements, Kunz believes that it is possible (more exactly and subtly than in the once much invoked postulate of an absolute answer to the question of human meaning) thus to conceive the divine personal Thou.

Heribert Mühlen, however, would not wish to consider God as the personal Thou over against man. In his analysis of the classical model of theism coming down from Aristotle and Aquinas, which Mühlen faults for its orientation to instrumentality (and therefore a 'reified' interpretament, a general thou-lessness),[26] he points out that God cannot exist in the same sense of 'thou' as one's fellow man. God is rather to be conceived as 'the condition of the possibility of Thou-encounter in general or of that *unlimited* thou which is to be met with in every encounter with one's fellow man, but never *as such* and without distinction from such an encounter.'[27]

Finally, W. Kerns does not see thought about God's personality as dependent on a theistic natural theology, but as reflection on the Judaeo-Christian revelation. To be sure, objections against the personality of God must be taken seriously, as when in the nineteenth century Strauss and Biedermann found it impossible to use the notion of person (marked as it was by application to finite spirit) to refer to God, and thereby to abstract from finiteness. In the twentieth century, Jaspers and Bloch see the notion of a personal God as a reification and finitization of the absolute. Kerns believes that it is possible to remove these objections by using the terms 'person' and 'personality' only analogously of God. Revelation bears witness to an active God; action is expressed in the functional analogy of man and God, but a functional analogy presupposes a structural analogy: 'Free, loving disposability for action, which is comprised in his actual acting, is God's personality.'[28]

## THREE CONSEQUENCES

At the end of this survey, it is impossible to cite any incontestable results of the critique of theism which might now be integrated into theology. But certain theoretical difficulties are obvious which could have an unfortunate effect on discourse on and practice in relation to God, because of a lack of critical reflection. Three such aporias will be raised now.

1. All attempts to revise theism or to supplant it by means of a new conceptuality fail without the vocabulary of the narrative and faith tradition. That is always true of at least one word: *God*. The non-theistic interpretaments considered have at least one feature in common with that conventional vocabulary: namely, they are analogies, and are therefore permanently in need of interpretation. That is evidently the case, for instance, with the personalistic 'absolute Thou', for there we must explain who the continually silent subject of that 'Thou' is, and to what extent he is not to be confused with a human thou. It is true also of the 'depth of being' or the 'ground of all being', where we must show why it or he is not a neutral quantity wholly contradictory to the history of human hope. In all instances, talk of God remains analogous. But the history of theism shows that criticism was voiced largely because the analogous nature of its vocabulary is not always, and not always adequately, explained by those who use it.

2. Great hermeneutical precision is required when discussing the divine attributes. R. Lay's thesis is that attributes can be postulated of God only in order to reject false ideas. Then the attributes ascribed to God would have a 'merely negative' significance.[29] Of the classical theological approaches (*affirmatio, negatio* and *eminentia*), only *negatio* would be legitimate. Analogous discourse about God could not be anything other than the negation of negative contents or names. This thesis is certainly too radical in regard to *affirmatio*. There are affirmative statements about God in which it is not apparent why they should lead one astray; as for instance the statement that God is love. However, each individual statement would have to be examined to show under what conditions of understanding it came about, and whether it is still possible to speak of a continuity of those conditions. When, for example, did the biblical usage 'pantocrator', which recalls the universal claim of the God of Israel,[30] change to talk about the Almighty, who can at all times realize everything that does not metaphysically contradict him? Did this change occur in social circumstances which allowed 'power' to be understood as positive? When the tenet of the 'almighty power' of God was handed down by the fourth Lateran Council and Vatican I as a formula without critical reflection, did the understanding

of power change so that the originally appropriate formula might well be misunderstood? Surely we now—in view of the fact that all power, ecclesiastical or secular, brings suffering and corrupts the power-holder —could find a more appropriate attribute in the powerlessness of the solidarity and compassion of God? Such questions ought to be asked, and asked most meticulously, about every divine attribute. To be sure, the mere insight that a magisterial formulation that once was correct can be falsified under altered conditions of understanding does not give us the right to use a new formula that would cancel the qualitative distinction between God and mankind.

3. In the discussion of theism, one often meets with the opinion that prayer is the test-case for the legitimacy and appropriateness of a specific idea and way of talking about God. This requires more exact inquiry where it is a question of the critical-instance prayer—petition. Is God still the God of men when petitionary prayer wholly loses meaning or becomes immanent therapy—mere self-expression? If God is a God who acts as spirit in the spirit of mankind, yet does not interfere in the physical processes of the world (which are under man's control), is it meaningful during a drought to ask for rain? If God is a God of all men, does it accord with his nature miraculously to heal this or that mortally ill individual, yet at the same time to abandon millions? Who would really want to be such an exception? The official prayers of the Church greatly influence notions of God, and theologians are right to demand great care from their composers and users. They should also draw attention to the fact that there is a way of praying that is neither the resigned acceptance of a forced destiny nor infantile illusion; it is the plaint of one who does not shake off God even though he cannot understand God and his behaviour. For those who prayed the psalms and for Jesus, lamentation in the face of the inconceivable was permissible. That is of course the strongest criticism of Christian theism.

*Translated by V. Green*

## Notes

1. See Dorothee Sölle's books (e.g. *Truth is Concrete* [London and New York, 1969]) for a very relevant account of these experiences.
2. Cf. W. Kern, 'A-theistisches Christentum?', in E. Coreth and J. B. Lotz (eds.), *Atheismus kritisch betrachtet* (Munich and Freiburg, 1971), pp. 143–71, esp. 56.

3. Cf. L. Scheffczyk, *Gott-loser Gottesglaube?* (Regensburg, 1974), p. 56.

4. See W. Kern, *op. cit.*, p. 147; M. Honecker, 'Gibt es eine nach-theistische Theologie?', in *Monatsschrift für Pastoraltheologie* 57 (1968), pp. 156–69, esp. 162; H. Ott, *Wirklichkeit und Glaube*, I (Zurich, 1966), p. 24.

5. The critique of theism is to be found primarily in P. Tillich, *The Courage to Be* (New York and London, 1953).

6. Cf. H.-M. Baumgartner, 'Sur la Conception de Dieu dans la Philosophie transcendentale', in *Archives de Philosophie* (1968), pp. 531–55; F. Wagner, *Der Gedanke der Persönlichkeit Gottes bei Fichte und Hegel* (Gütersloh, 1971).

7. Tillich's idea was widely distributed through J. A. T. Robinson's *Honest to God* (London, 1962), which offered a simplified version of it. For a more philosophic analysis, see L. Dewart, *The Future of Belief* (New York and London, 1967).

8. Cf. R. Bultmann, 'Der Gottesgedanke und der moderne Mensch', in *Zeitschrift für Theologie und Kirche* 60 (1963), pp. 335–48; *id.*, 'Die protestantische Theologie und der Atheismus', *ibid.*, 68 (1971), pp. 376–80, esp. 378.

9. Among them is certainly W. Pannenberg, *Grundfragen systematischer Theologie* (Göttingen, 1967), pp. 361–98; *id.*, *Gottesgedanke und menschliche Freiheit* (Göttingen, 1972), pp. 29–47.

10. R. Bultmann, 'Die protestantische Theologie,' pp. 379ff.

11. H. Braun, *Gesammelte Studien zum Neuen Testament und seiner Umwelt* (Tübingen, second ed., 1967), pp. 324–41, esp. 341.

12. Dorothee Sölle's theology is not only negation and destruction; its sensitivity to suffering is noteworthy.

13. D. Sölle, *Das Recht, ein anderer zu werden* (Neuwied, 1971), p. 47.

14. U. Hedinger, *Wider die Versöhnung Gottes mit dem Elend* (Zurich, 1972).

15. H. Gollwitzer, *Von der Stellvertretung Gottes* (Munich, 1967), pp. 132–40, esp. 135.

16. H. Ott, *Gott* (Stuttgart, 1971), pp. 10–16.

17. H. Ott, *Wirklichkeit und Glaube*, I, p. 23.

18. H. Ott, *ibid.*, II, p. 178.

19. H. Ott, *Gott*, p. 12; *Wirklichkeit und Glaube*, I, pp. 294, 307–10.

20. J. Moltmann, *The Crucified God* (London and New York, 1973).

21. J. Moltmann, *ibid.*

22. J. Moltmann, *ibid.* See also the Japanese theologian K. Kitamori's *Theology of the Pain of God* (London, 1970).

23. Karl Rahner's reference to God's capability of suffering (inasmuch as God suffers and dies in someone other than himself) in *Schriften* IV (Eng. trans., *Theological Investigations*, Vol. 4) is the only constructive contribution to the aporia of the unchangeability of God in this century, whereas Hans Küng in *Menschwerdung Gottes* (Freiburg, 1970) offers a mere account of the known problem. See for the North American contributions, P. A. M. Schoonenberg, 'Process or History in God?', in *Louvain Studies* (1974), pp. 303–19.

24. See on Rahner's theology, K. P. Fischer, *Der Mensch als Geheimnis* (Freiburg, 1974).

25. E. Kunz, *Christentum ohne Gott?* (Frankfurt, 1971).

26. H. Mühlen, *Die abendländische Seinsfrage als der Tod Gottes und der Aufgang einer neuen Gotteserfahrung* (Paderborn, 1968).

27. H. Mühlen, *ibid.*, p. 28; cf. also, R. Lay, *Zukunft ohne Religion?* (Olten and Freiburg, 1970).

28. W. Kern, *op. cit.*, pp. 163ff.

29. R. Lay, *op. cit.*

30. *Theologisches Wörterbuch zum Neuen Testament*, III, pp. 913ff.

# PART II

*The 'Personal Divine' and the 'Impersonal Divine'*

Peter Nemeshegyi

# Concepts and Experiences
# of God in Asia

'THE transient visitor to Asia thinks he understands everything. If he stays longer, he feels he understands nothing. And if he spends a very long time there, he will understand a little'.[1] How true! The author of this article has been living in Asia for more than twenty years. Does that entitle him to include himself in the third category quoted above? Be that as it may, he certainly does not feel he can claim to understand everything. At most, a certain amount. But what he does understand fills him with amazement and astonishment. Asia is a world unto itself; vast, deep and extraordinarily varied: a world in which men have spent thousands of years grappling with the deepest problems of existence. Obviously, not everything in Asia commands our admiration. But there is something remarkable in the Asiatic search for God, and this phenomenon is worthy of our closest attention.

There is no such thing as a standardized Asian concept of God. In his excellent book *Ways of Thinking of Eastern Peoples, India, China, Tibet and Japan* (Honolulu, 1964), the eminent Japanese Buddhologist, H. Nakamura, produces ample evidence to prove that fundamental contradictions exist between the thought processes of the major far eastern cultures. For example, the individual nature of Indian and Chinese thinking can be characterized as follows:

THE INDIAN

1. emphasizes the general, the spiritual;
2. prefers abstract and negative ways of expression;

THE CHINESE

1. emphasizes the individual, the material;
2. prefers concrete imagery and diagrams;

37

3. is convinced of the ultimate unity of all reality;

3. delights in the multiplicity of individual phenomena;

4. considers reality as something static;

4. is interested in history;

5. despises the material world;

5. loves nature and elegant social intercourse;

6. is interested in the mental processes;

6. is interested in a well-ordered society;

7. is disposed towards speculation and religion.

7. is by nature practical and utilitarian.

India and China are therefore totally different. And Japan is another world altogether. My aim here is to examine the paths taken by these three distinct worlds in their search for God.

### THE JOYFUL EXPERIENCE OF ONENESS

India today is still a deeply religious country. Daily prayer, countless rituals, great religious festivals, pilgrimages, etc., dominate the entire life of both individual and society. Even today, hundreds of thousands of individuals who have renounced everything in their search for God are still living in the temples, settlements and woods, or spend their lives wandering from place to place. 'Hinduism embraces fetishists, those who worship village gods . . . those who believe in demons, those who venerate tools and instruments, or rather, the spirits present in them, as well as those who perform crude rituals. At the other extreme, it includes ascetics, those who devote their lives to a personalized God in a spirit of burning love and fervent renunciation or those who seek their salvation by means of meditation or profound philosophical or theological systems'.[2]

This outpouring of religious feeling is rooted in a mystical experience of oneness. Although that experience is regarded as particularly important in Hinduism, it is by no means limited to that religion. Throughout history, men and women have had a similar experience. I should like to quote a few examples of such experiences, beginning with two texts from the Indian classics which appear to have been written as a result of such an experience: 'Smaller than the smallest, yet greater than the greatest, Atman conceals himself in the depths of all creatures. Whoever has renounced his own will may contemplate him, and all pain then dissolves. Through the bounty of the creator he contemplates the greatness of Atman.'[3] And: 'When a man denies himself, when he renounces all power, pride, lust, anger and greed, when he no longer thinks of himself, when he is at peace with himself, then he is able to become one with Brahman. And having become one with Brahman, his soul is calm. He has no more griefs or desires. At one with all things he receives the greatest love for Me. And through this love he knows Me, as I am. He perceives how great I am, and who I am. And as soon as he perceives Me, he becomes one with Me.'[4]

The two texts that follow were written not so long ago by two Japanese women. Both were brought up without religion, but were finally led to the Christian faith by the experiences they describe. The first report is an extract from a letter addressed to me. The experience described here took place about fifty years ago. "One day, when I was ten years old, tired of playing with my dolls, I went into our garden and sat down on a bench. All of a sudden, an immense light surrounded me, a light from another world, streaming and yet soft. Not only I, but also the trees and the mountain were bathed in this light. And suddenly I understood that a wonderful being exists who surpasses everything else in the world. I also understood that this being is eternal love. And it embraced my small heart completely. I don't know how long this state of ecstasy lasted, but when I came to myself again, my beloved dolls and everything else in this world seemed like ashes or the spray on the water. Ten years after this experience I heard a Christian teaching about God and immediately knew that it was he whom I had experienced that day. There is no word that can describe him adequately.'

The second report comes from one of my students. Brought up without religion, she had suffered much. One evening she was close to despair. Then, as she was climbing wearily up to her home, she happened to look up at the starry sky. And then it happened: 'I felt as if the whole sky opened itself to me. It was as if the whole sky existed for me alone! Every star was ablaze with light, bright and large and unbelievably clear. All the stars seemed to whisper "Yes, you may live! Just as you are, you are worthy of life. Just as you are, I love you"'. The experience overwhelmed her, and six months later she asked to be baptized.

From these and countless other texts we can characterize the fundamental mystical experience as follows:

1. The experience is sudden and is received as a favour.
2. It is an experience of oneness with the divine.
3. Awareness of time and space disappears. There is a glimpse of eternity.
4. The experience induces a deep sense of joy and endless peace. All problems and doubts vanish. The person concerned feels free.
5. He feels protected by an eternal, merciful love.
6. The experience is indescribable.
7. The experience causes a fundamental change in the lifestyle of the

individual concerned. He becomes friendly, humble, selfless, peaceable. He loves everything and everyone with the love that he has experienced.

An experience of this nature, repeated again and again, is the living spring of Hinduism. Of the characteristics of this experience quoted above two are particularly important: (a) The experience of oneness; (b) The experience of protective divine grace.

The experience of oneness is especially emphasized by Indian mystics. But the experience of divine grace is by no means lacking in the Indian tradition. Even Sankara, the system which most emphasizes this basic oneness, is not called a 'doctrine of oneness' (monism), but *Advaita* or 'doctrine of non-duality'. Brahman and man are not separate, but that does not mean that they are simply one and the same. A favourite Buddhist expression for the relationship between 'suchness' (Tathatā) and the phenomenal world is 'not-two, not-one'. Even greater stress is laid on the 'way of devotion' (bhakti-marga) followed by the large majority of Hindus, which can be described as the devotional encounter with the God who loves us, while forgetting oneself in the ecstasy of love. For example, the famous poet and mystic Rabindranāth Tagore (1861–1941) sees 'God through human eyes as a loving, merciful and benevolent being constantly communicating with human beings in need of help'.[5]

It is, however, true to say that the experience of non-duality is particularly strong in the Indian concept of God, even in the theistically inclined forms of *bhakti* and above all in the quiet meditation of the jnāna (wisdom). This factor has caused many, in particular Protestant, theologians such as A. Ritschl, N. Söderblom, E. Brunner, H. Kraemer, and so on, to make a distinction between the 'prophetic religion' of the Bible and the 'mystical religion' of the Far East.

THE PROPHET

1. encounters the living, almighty, supreme, "totally other" God;
2. prays to God and reveals his truth;
3. believes in the importance of the world of creation;
4. is filled with holy wrath against sin, especially the worship of false idols;

THE MYSTIC

1. experiences oneness with the silent absolute;
2. knows that silence is the only adequate way of praising the ineffable;
3. regards the world as an illusion;
4. adopts a peaceful attitude to all beings, no matter what stage they have reached in the process of self-realization, and is tolerant towards all forms of religion;

| | |
|---|---|
| 5. lives by placing his trust in faith; | 5. lives by self-evident experience; |
| 6. strives towards the future promised by God; | 6. is content with the joyful present; |
| 7. knows that he stands under God's judgment. | 7. is sure of the freedom he has already attained. |

These theologians consider the two basic forms of religion outlined above to be irreconcilable. The choice has to be made: either faith or mysticism. For, in his sublime way, the mystic commits the original sin of wanting to be God.

There is certainly some truth in this dichotomy. But it must strike us as odd that this same antithesis is propounded by members of various eastern religions, but with the evaluation reversed. Hence they see the monotheist as fanatical, self-righteous and arrogant, with his condemnatory superiority and intolerance. All these, together with the Inquisition, the Crusades and the religious wars, are contrasted with the tolerant, peaceful, life-protecting Orient which aims solely to shelter and elucidate.

Such antitheses can usefully demonstrate the extremes that can be reached by either type of religion if it sets itself up as absolute. In my view, they in no way prove that prophetic faith and mystical experience are mutually exclusive. On the contrary, it would seem that they need and complement each other. The great Catholic tradition of Christianity, especially in the eastern Church, has always valued the mystical experience highly. It played an essential role in shaping Christianity, drawing on the writings of Paul and John and enriched by the neo-Platonism associated with Indian religion. Where mysticism flourishes, it nurtures the fruits of humility, awareness of the inadequacy of all purely human formulae, a sense of calm joy, peace in God, and the immersion of self in that eternal love which 'moves the sun and the stars' (Dante) illuminating everything with its brilliance. Where mysticism is missing, monotheism becomes what Comte described regretfully as 'the Western sickness'.

But the mystic type of religion also needs the prophetic. Some depth-psychological research as well as experiences induced by drugs have shown that psychological states very similar to the mystical experience of non-duality can exist without having any religious truth or value. Aldous Huxley, whose glowing account of his mystical experiences induced by mescalin caused such a stir, made the noteworthy confession on his death bed that it was an insight, but at the same time the most dangerous of errors, inasmuch as one was worshipping oneself.[6] Self-adulation of this kind indicates pride and can lead all too easily to moral irresponsibility and indifference to the needs of others. The subjective individual experience is by no means a sufficient justification of its religious authenticity. In the words of Christ: 'You will know them by their fruits'. But just what these good fruits are is shown authoritatively by prophetic religion. First, in that it culminates in the person of Jesus Christ, and second, in that it regards the absolute love of God as indivisible from the attentive, concrete, universal love of mankind. Divine revelation, testified to by the 'cloud of witnesses' (Hebrews 12:1) and borne out by the faith of the people of God, offers us a safer stronghold among a multiplicity of subjective experiences.

I therefore feel that any scheme that plays off the personalized God against an unpersonal absolute, or the transcendental God against an immanent principle, is a non-viable simplification. The formulae of non-differentiation used by mystical religions are often of an ethical nature, or they are double negatives intended to suggest the mystery of eternity incomprehensible to a thought process which contrasts subject with object. These formulae are only unacceptable when they attempt to express a monistic identity. And that applies not only to prophetic religions flourishing in Asia, to Mohammedanism, and to the very old forms of Christianity still active in many places, but equally to *bhakti* piety in Hinduism and *boddhisattva* piety in Buddhism. A one-sided mystical doctrine of non-duality would also result in an over-emphasis on the characteristics of Indian thought mentioned earlier on, and hence neglect the more universal aspects of Chinese thought.

On the other hand, the emphasis on non-duality in Eastern mysticism certainly has a most important contribution to make to a deeper consideration of this factor in all religions. God is transcendent, but he is also immanent. He is ineffable, sublime, and yet 'In him we live and move and have our being' (Acts 17:28). He is immanent by means of creation and, more fundamentally still, by means of his free, merciful revelation to us. If man is not baptized in God, his religion is reduced to a hoarse cry, uneasy activism, the trimming of worldly aims with religious slogans, to a hollow vessel without substance, to a thin vein of water which sinks into the sand. Man can only find himself if he loses himself in the endless stream of divine love flowing through him.

## GOD AS THE SOURCE OF HUMAN CHARITY

Any discussion of the Asiatic concept of God should not overlook the fact that a considerable proportion of Asians still practise an extremely primitive polytheism. Its simple folk religions teem with gods and spirits, all too often conceived as malevolent, jealous, revengeful, contentious beings. Knowing the feelings of insecurity and fear instilled by belief in such beings, it is very easy to understand why, for example, K. Uchimura, one of the most important Japanese Christians of the Meiji period, describes the sense of liberation he experienced at his conversion so movingly; he felt himself finally freed from the crippling, fear-inducing throngs of gods who uphold an unjust social order and impose absurd obligations. The great achievement of revealed religion is that it liberates men from the dominance of gods who are nothing more than the projection of human fear, greed, ignorance and so on. But one other form of religion, if not as effective as revealed religion, has helped to purify religion in Asia, namely the Chinese doctrine of heaven.

The Chinese are extremely sensitive to beauty and the judicious ordering of nature, and towards justice, cleanliness and a rational social order. The great achievement of Chinese religion is that it succeeds in combining these two spheres by anchoring them in one fundamental principle.

The moral doctrines of K'ung-tsŭ (Confucius) are a good example of this. Confucius postulates a very upright morality when he says: 'My whole doctrine can be summarized in a single phrase: strive for perfection and love your fellow-men as you love yourself' (*Analects* IV, 15). 'Treat others as you would be treated by them' (VI, 28). 'The noble man regards all men who live between the four seas as his brothers' (XII, 5). 'The perfect man, or one who strives for perfection, will never save his life if it means violating that perfection. In certain circumstances he will sacrifice his life in order to follow the path of goodness' (XV, 8).

In Confucius' thought this morality is based on the 'will of heaven' (XVI, 8). 'Heaven rewards those who follow reason, and it punishes those who act against reason' (III, 13). To be good is to imitate heaven.

'Heaven' is the source of the benevolent natural order which embraces all things. From heaven is derived the social order which is not disfigured by lust, greed, dispute, violence, injustice, and so on, but which is guided and ennobled by order, mutual help, goodwill, good manners, integrity, art, knowledge and so on. The fact that for hundreds of years the Chinese empire was governed by a class of scholars whose competency had been proved by means of rigorous examinations, rather than by the hereditary aristocracy, the chief priests or a plutocracy, is a remarkable consequence of this philosophy.

As is well known, there is no consistent interpretation of 'heaven' in the history of Chinese thought. Chinese differs fundamentally from Indian thought in tending to a worldly, somewhat materialistic interpretation. Yet even to those who identified heaven with the material vault of heaven it remained—to quote Eliade—hierophantic. But other Chinese thinkers regard heaven as a personalized being to whose benevolent will both the world and mankind are subject. Matteo Ricci was not alone in considering this concept derived from the Chinese classics as the more primitive. Contemporary thinkers such as Seung-Kook Lew, Professor at the Confucian Sung Kyun Kwan University in Seoul, are also of the same opinion. However, it must be admitted that the Chinese God of heaven does not make such a great impact on men's minds as the God of revealed religion. But this is not necessarily a shortcoming. In order to demonstrate this, we must consider another important form of Chinese religion: namely, Taoism.

Confucianism advocates culture and socially useful activity. Taoism concerns itself with the simplicity of nature and 'not doing'. But this 'not doing' is by no means to be equated with inertia. 'Taoism is eternal not doing, and therefore nothing remains undone' (Lao-tse, *Tao-Te-King*, 37). It creates, but does not possess. Hence the saying: 'To create and not possess, to act and not set any store by, to maintain and not dominate, that is true virtue' (51). K'ung-tsǔ teaches that "one should be kind to those who are good, but that one should only be just to those who are bad" (XIV, 36). But the holy man of the Lao-tsǔ says: "I am good to those who are good. But I am also good to those who are not good. Virtue is goodness" (49). Tao is like water; it activates, nourishes and creates through its maternal weakness which in the final analysis conquers all force and virility. To the individual who in this way perceives the fundamental reality suffusing all things a world of undreamed of beauty, delicacy and depth reveals itself. G. Béky writes aptly that 'the delicate pictures of Chinese and Japanese art, the almost supernatural subtleties of their painting, suggesting something inexpressible with a minimum of effort or materials, the matchless colour combinations of the kimono, the superlatively delicate lustre of Chinese porcelain, the hazy perfection of a Zen painting, and indeed many other phenomena in Chinese and Japanese history are unthinkable without Tao. They are all moulded by the spirit of unreality. They are all permeated by the subtle strength of Tao, the deeply feminine'.[7]

The Chinese tradition has two great religious concepts to offer humanity. The first, Confucianism, stemming from and imitating the original, calm, beautiful world order, humanitarian, thankful, harmonious, and avoiding all excess. And on the other hand, Taoism, clinging to the maternal warmth of the inexpressible, all-embracing primary cause.

China today is obviously a totally different world. No society has ever broken so completely with its past. Maoism asserts itself as an extremely puritanical, militant, absolute and exclusive religion of materialism. Is this the way to bring Asia into the modern world? At any rate Japan, the most highly developed country in Asia, has chosen a different way. What, then, is the contemporary Japanese attitude to religion?

### SMILING HARMONY

Japan is a living museum for the religious scientist. All forms of religion seem to be flourishing there, from the most primitive Shamanism to the most subtle methods of meditation; from the noisy popular temple festival to the solemn peace of the shrines. The scope of this article is very limited, but I hope that the following examples will throw some light on the vital Japanese contribution to our knowledge of God.

The most important festival in Japan is the New Year festival. Everyone returns to his native town. Everything is given a special cleaning. Special New Year dishes are prepared. All factories, offices and schools close. All debts are paid. People exchange countless New Year cards, of greeting and gratitude. On New Year's Eve everyone dons his or her most beautiful kimono and makes a pilgrimage to a shrine. Endless streams of people wend their way to the Shintoist or Buddhist temples, each standing for a moment in front of the main temple with bowed head and folded hands. Then, composing themselves, they bow, cast a donation in the alms box and return home with a light heart. The weather is always beautiful. The New Year's sun rises large and red above the horizon and is greeted by millions. After a happy, chatty family meal, visits are made to friends and relations.

It is almost impossible for anyone who has not experienced the Japanese New Year to appreciate the deep feeling of universal harmony that pervades the country at this time. The tangible multiplicity of the world manifesting itself in beautiful forms seems to be embraced by a gentle, smiling eternity. Were one to ask the countless pilgrims to whom they prayed at the shrine and whether they believe in the Shinto god or Buddha worshipped in the relevant shrine, most would not be able to give a definite answer. For what moves the Japanese soul most deeply is not an objective, clearly conceptualized divinity, but rather that something forming the endless basis of all reality and preceding any subject-object differentiation. This something is embodied in all the countless gods—in the case of Shinto, they number eight million. To identify this something, it is not simply a matter of lifting the veil from the object. Rather, the veil lies close round the heart of the subject. But when, in the emotion of the moment, this veil vanishes, the individual becomes aware of his union with the source of all life, the keynote of all harmony.

The Japanese are not disposed towards metaphysical speculation, renouncing the world or lifelong asceticism. Japan is the only country where nearly all Buddhist monks marry. The Japanese prefer simplicity in matters of religion. For this reason all the great Buddhist reformers in medieval Japan chose one single element on which to concentrate. Hence Dōgen (1200–1253) emphasized meditation in the lotus posture; Nichiren (1222–1282) stressed the recitation of the first words of the lotus sutra; while Hōnen (1133–1212) and Shinran (1173–1262) chose as their focal point the pious invocation of Amida. In Japan, Buddhism develops into belief in the mercy of a redeemer. In the teaching of Shinran, this doctrine of mercy is taken to the extreme. 'Even the good will be born anew in the Pure Land, the paradise of Amida. How much more so the wicked!' Even the 'good' who place their trust not in Amida's mercy but in their own deeds will be saved by him. Hence how much more so the wicked who acknowledge their unworthiness. Even the gravest sins are not excluded from this forgiveness. But for salvation it is not imperative to appeal explicitly to Amida, for Amida redeems all. At the moment of death he gathers all to his being.

In no other country has Buddhism, which in its original forms promised nirvana only to monks devoting themselves to the ascetic life, developed into such an optimistic doctrine based on faith and mercy. Is this not perhaps to be attributed to the fact that the Japanese is intuitively convinced of the gentle, loving, all-embracing, expiatory harmony of all existence?

The absence of metaphysics and revealed religion and the consequent lack of objective norms have, however, led to a number of misconceptions in Japanese religion. One such weakness that manifests itself in social terms is the way the Japanese attribute what amounts to absolute importance to defined social relationships. This has led to scrupulous group egotism, absolute feudalism, aggressive nationalism, and in the religious sphere to schisms and passionately antagonistic sects. The significance of the hundreds of flourishing 'new religions' is to be sought above all in the social bonds they symbolize. For they bring support, confidence, peace and hope to the individual in the urban wilderness.

Japanese religion has not constructed any major system of thought. But it has achieved a great deal in practical terms. For example, peaceful meditation in the lotus posture; gardening, the creation of a small, peaceful world of beauty, not merely to be looked at and admired, but to inspire the individual both emotionally and existentially to meditate; the mastery of the paint-brush fusing spontaneity and control; and archery, where the arrow hits the target when the marksman no longer desires to do so, when he experiences a sense of oneness with the target. For the Japanese these are just some of the ways of attaining a direct union with the primary cause, the source of all creation, holding and releasing all things in a profusion of beauty. All life passes away speedily and there is no answer to the mystery of creation. But since the world contains so much that is good and beautiful, it must in the final analysis have its origins in goodness and beauty. The Japanese consciousness, it seems to me, derives from this unarticulated but strongly emotive belief. This perhaps explains why Mozart's music means so much to the Japanese.

### SUMMARY

God, the mystical, joyful experience of oneness. God, the source of humanity among men. God, the mercifully smiling harmony. These are the three major aspects of the conception and experience of God with which the Far East has lived for thousands of years and continues to live today. None of these aspects contradicts in any sense the God of Christian revelation. He is the One who unifies everything in himself. He is the love which embraces all things. He is the keynote of beauty which reveals itself in a myriad of ways in creation. He manifests himself in Jesus, the *universale concretum* (H. Urs von Balthasar). He is the 'note sung by our harmony' (Ignatius of Antioch). Our counterparts in Asia can help us to find him over and over again. 'For he is infinite in order that, even when found, he must be sought eternally' (Augustine).

*Translated by Sarah Twohig*

## Notes

1. O. Wolff, *Anders an Gott glauben* (Stuttgart, 1969), p. 92.
2. Jan Gonda, *Die Religionen Indiens,* I, *Veda und älterer Hinduismus* (Stuttgart, 1960), p. 343.
3. *Katha Upanishad*, 2, 20–23.
4. *Bhagavad-Gita*, 18, 53–55.
5. Jan Gonda, *op. cit.*, II, *Der jüngere Hinduismus* (Stuttgart, 1963), p. 330.
6. Laura Archera Huxley, *This Timeless Moment* (New York, 1968), pp. 268–69.
7. G. Béky, *Die Welt des Tao* (Munich, 1972), p. 188.

Manfred Vogel

# Some Reflections on Jewish Concepts of God

OUR subject-matter is in the domain of theology: that is, in the rational interpretative superstructure that a religious tradition provides for its faith. As such, speaking of 'concepts' in the plural rather than in the singular is accurate, for no concrete historical religious tradition is monolithic in its intellectual understanding of its faith. A historical religious tradition is bound by common memories, symbols, celebrations, rituals and texts, but it almost invariably presents a spectrum of views when it comes to interpreting their meaning and significations. This is true particularly of Judaism where the thrust of the structure of faith is towards the deed rather than the intellectual confession, towards *Halacha* rather than dogma, and where consequently the striving for uniformity is directed towards *Halachic* practice, whereas a fairly wide leeway is tolerated as regards the philosophic-theological interpretation of the faith. Still, I would want to argue that amidst the variety of views there is a view (particularly as regards the concept of God which is so fundamental a concept in the structure of faith) that is normative. (It is normative not only because it is a distinctive, widely and consistently-held view but because where different views are held, they are mitigated as much as possible to meet the requirements of this view.)

This normative view is usually presented as asserting (*a*) that God is one—one in the sense of there being only one divine being (arithmetical oneness), of his uniqueness and of the uncompounded, simple constitution of his being; (*b*) that God is transcendent to man and the world, that in principle neither apotheosis nor incarnation is ever possible: in short, that the view of God is thoroughly theistic; (*c*) that God by his very essence is ethical; and (*d*) that the relation of man to God is a relation of prayer, or address, and not of use and manipulation. But the very essence of the normative view lies in the assertion that God *qua* ultimate being is a person—a living being endowed with awareness and the spontaneity of free will. As ultimate, man encounters consciousness, concern, and not impersonal power moving blindly by inexorable necessity. God is encountered as a Thou, not as an it.

## THE ESSENCE OF THE NORMATIVE VIEW: GOD AS A THOU

With the exception of the 'arithmetical oneness' characterization which follows from the view of God being ultimate rather than from his being a Thou (ultimacy necessarily implicates arithmetical oneness and as such, indeed, an it-God when viewed as ultimate would equally be arithmetically one), all the abovementioned and the many other, albeit less fundamental, characterizations of the normative view not mentioned here would follow necessarily from the inner logic of the view of God as Thou and would receive their rationale from it.

Hence the characterization of the being of God as uncompounded and simple (that is, undifferentiated and indivisible) is necessitated by this Thouness. For division and multiplicity are feasible only with respect to matter, to corporeality, to a being extended in the space-time continuum. These are all inescapable determinants of the manifestation of power and therefore of an It-being. A Thou-God, however, being the expression of consciousness and not of power is by its very constitution not subject to these determinants and consequently compoundness and differentiation are in principle inapplicable to it.

Similarly, a Thou-God is necessarily unique inasmuch as every thou is by its very constitution necessarily unique. Each person *qua* person is unique—non-duplicable and irreplaceable. Uniqueness here is not merely quantitative and contingent; it is qualitative and essential. Each thou-being, in contradistinction to an it-being, is constituted as a unique being. As such, uniqueness is applicable not only to God but to any being that is a thou and is grounded in the very constitution of the being as a thou. This is not the case in the it-realm. An it-being is not constituted as unique and consequently when uniqueness is applied to an it-God, its status and rationale are quite different. It cannot be grounded in its very constitution as an it but only in such distinctions which are ultimately reducible to the infinite-finite distinction—a distinction which, in the last analysis, is merely quantitative. As such, uniqueness here can only be a uniqueness of quantity or configuration but not, as is the case with the thou-being, one of essence.

These distinctions are further clarified and buttressed by the following all-important characterization of the Thou-God as necessarily theistic in contradistinction to the it-God which necessarily gravitates towards being pantheistic. A Thou-God is necessarily theistic because he is a being-of-consciousness, and consciousness by its essence is always and necessarily structured as a consciousness of something, thus necessarily implicating a something, an other, and a 'gap', an over-againstness, between itself and this other. A Thou-God, therefore, is a being who necessarily implicates an other (e.g., man, the world) over-against himself. But otherness and over-againstness necessarily implicate the theistic relation of transcendence, of beyondness—one necessarily transcends an other which is over-against it. A Thou-God, therefore, by virtue of his being a being-of-consciousness, necessarily implicates an other over against himself and consequently is necessarily a theistic, transcending God. Pantheism cannot provide the relational matrix for a Thou-God. For pantheism is based on the oneness of a continuum whereas consciousness is based on the duality of an over-againstness. Consciousness cannot be constituted within a continuum, and consequently a Thou-God cannot be, in principle, embedded within a continuum: which is to say, that in principle he cannot be pantheistic. A Thou-God linked to pantheism is possible only at the price of inconsistency. No wonder that normative Judaism has consistently and strenuously rejected pantheism. (The situation is reversed, however, regarding the it-God, the ultimate being-of-power. The inner logic of the it domain necessarily pulls the it-God towards pantheism. For power in manifesting itself constitutes itself as a continuum, and consequently the ensuing oneness does not disintegrate to a being-of-power; indeed, in their essence the manifold beings of power are but various manifestations, differentiated merely by the degree of power manifested, of a single, all-inclusive being of power. In such a context where a continuum and quantitative gradation inextricably characterize the being-of-power, the it-God *qua* ultimate must manifest maximal power which, in turn, requires that the totality of manifested power be included in it: that is, that it be a pantheistic God.)

The case for the remaining two characterizations can be made briefly. Ethical considerations can be applied only to a Thou-God. For only a being endowed with awareness and free will can carry responsibility and therefore be subject to ethical demands and judgment. As against this, it simply does not make sense to raise the ethical in regard to an it-God, a being devoid of awareness and acting blindly with inexorable necessity. Only in regard to a Thou-God can one ask: 'Is the judge of all the earth not to do justice?' or raise the Jobian challenge; it is senseless to do so in regard to blind power. Similarly, addressing the other in the second person is feasible only in regard to a being endowed with awareness: that is, a Thou-God; to address a being devoid of awareness, an it-God, is simply senseless. One can relate to an it-God only in the third person—describing, manipulating, predicting (in religious discourse, magic and divination), relations which are excluded by the very essence of the ontological constitution of a thou.

## DOES A THOU VIEW IMPLY AN UTILITARISTIC INDIVIDUALISM?

Clearly, in the whole question of formulating the concept of God, the fundamental parting of the way—the basic alternative—is whether God is viewed as Thou or as it. All other issues are ultimately clarified by reference to one or the other of these basic characterizations and the inner logic they respectively imply. Let us briefly illustrate this by referring to one of the questions posed for this issue of *Concilium*: 'Does a personalist-theistic in contradistinction to an impersonalist-pantheistic view imply an utilitaristic individualism?'

What are we to say to this? First, our analysis above should clearly justify the linking of the personalist view, i.e., the Thou-God, with theism and the impersonalist view, i.e., the it-God, with pantheism. And, as to the substance of the answer, to be properly grounded it must follow the implications of the Thou-God and the it-God respectively. Here, we must grant that a Thou-God does indeed imply individualism. A Thou-God requires that man in relation to him, i.e., that man in the authentic expression of his being, be also a thou; and as thou, man necessarily preserves his particularity, uniqueness and irreplaceability over-against his fellow man, nature and God; the necessarily implied theism implies in turn individualism. On this score, the it-God in its implication of pantheism does indeed abrogate the possibility of individualism. Ultimately, all individuation is illusory—all individuals are in essence one and the same. Thus, ontologically speaking, while the theistic Thou-God necessitates individualism, the pantheistic it-God excludes it.

It is a different matter, however, as regards the utilitaristic contention, namely, the contention that the Thou-God in precipitating individuation precipitates also an utilitaristic relationship between the individuals (being distinct and unique they would be self-centred and utilitaristic in relating to the other). Granted, the thou-individual by his very constitution can arise only in relation (in relation to another thou), and consequently the thou-individual is indeed always and necessarily in relation; he cannot be self-enclosed, in isolation, 'monadic'. The thou must be embedded in a relation but not every relation would do. The thou can arise only in a relation of address—of calling forth, of confirming, the other as thou. The thou can arise only in a relation of giving, of self-impartation (either in the form of self-presentation or of challenge) and such a relation cannot be self-centred, egotistical; in its very essence it is other-centred. Furthermore, the calling forth, the confirming is of the other in its otherness which means that the thou can arise only in relating to the other as an end-in-itself, as a subject; by its very constitution it cannot relate to the other as a means, as an object. But this clearly implies that a thou cannot subsist in an utilitaristic relation which is based on relating to the other as a means.

The thou cannot be constituted as a being-in-itself or as a being-for-itself. By its very essence it is constituted as a being-towards-another and for-another and as such its relation can be neither self-centred nor utilitaristic. The theistic Thou-God view does indeed precipitate individuation, but it is an individuation that necessarily implies communion —caring and responsibility for the other in his otherness.

Strange as it may seem, it is the pantheistic it-God view which, although abrogating ontological individualism, can nonetheless give rise to a self-centred and utilitaristic relating. Briefly stated, the rationale for this is as follows: in this view individuation is ultimately only apparent. Ultimately, there is only one all-encompassing being. Precisely speaking, therefore, there can be no other-centred relation here. For the all-encompassing being has no other over against it; and the apparent individuals are all but constituents of one and the same being and, therefore, no genuine otherness exists here either—all action of the apparent individual, both on behalf of himself and on behalf of the other, is ultimately one and the same, i.e., action on behalf of the one, all-encompassing being. As such also, since there is no genuine otherness, there can be no utilitaristic action either. But on a relative basis, from the viewpoint of the apparent individual, his relation to other apparent individuals would tend to be self-centred and utilitaristic. For the all-encompassing being of which the apparent individual is but a manifestation is an it-being, a being-of-power, and consequently the apparent individual would manifest the characterizations of a being-of-power, the essential characterization being self-aggrandizement towards the concentration of maximal power. A being-of-power is 'imperialistic', striving to increase the manifestation of power in itself to the maximum (hence the tendency to pantheism). It is thus constituted as a being-for-itself, and consequently its relation to all other entities is self-centred and utilitaristic; that is, using the other as a means to increase its manifestation of power (the utilitaristic relation being further encouraged by the fact that the apparent individual is ultimately devoid of a distinct, unique reality of his own and therefore can be easily reduced to a means). Hence, in the pantheistic it-God view there are two considerations pulling in opposite directions. The it-dimension pulls towards a self-centred utilitaristic relation; the pantheistic-dimension pulls towards its abrogation.

## VIEWS WHICH IMPLICATE A PANTHEISTIC IT-GOD

I have contended that the view of God as a theistic Thou-God is normative and deeply embedded in Judaism. The overwhelming witness of the Bible (excepting possibly Wisdom literature) and of rabbinic literature clearly testifies to this. But, as I have also noted above, no historical religious tradition is monolithic. Not surprisingly, we encounter variations and differences in the further elaboration of this basic view. What is somewhat more surprising, however, is the fact that we also encounter views which implicate a pantheistic it-God.

Most of the philosophic formulations within Judaism (e.g., Aristotelianism and neo-Platonism in the Middle Ages or idealism and naturalism in modern times) implicate an it-God. This is understandable. For, inasmuch as man is its starting-point and reason is its ultimate criterion, the philosophic enterprise leads to an it-God. The philosophic enterprise, by its very essence, is description, demonstration and evaluation, and as such its object, for instance, God, is necessarily an it-being. But although the God of Jewish philosophy is, in the last analysis, definitely an it-God, the interesting aspect of this enterprise lies in the attempts made to ascribe characterizations of the Thou-God to the it-God and in the glossing over of the problematic implications of the it-God. See for example the sustained efforts by medieval Jewish Aristotelianism to ascribe providence to a God viewed as First Cause or the strong emphasis by nineteenth-century Jewish idealism on the ethical and free-will aspects of the divine viewed as Spirit (although viewed as Spirit the divine here is nevertheless, in the last analysis, an it-God, as is the view of God as a First Cause). By the same token, see the efforts of Jewish neo-Platonism to gloss over and conceal the necessary pantheistic implications of its position, or the marked preference of nineteenth-century Jewish philosophy for Kant and the later Schelling (where a theistic dimension is present) over undiluted Hegelianism (where an uncompromised pantheism is expressed). Clearly, even in formulations where the view of God is unmistakenly that of an it-God, the impact of the normative view of a Thou-God is strongly felt.

An even more striking and intriguing instance of this phenomenon is encountered in Jewish mysticism which, by the way, pervades Judaism much more extensively and significantly than the philosophic enterprise. Jewish mysticism is an instance of the universal phenomenon of mysticism and as such it partakes of the structure universally characteristic of mystical phenomena. The essential thrust of this structure is a striving for oneness. For mysticism the ultimate predicament lies in separation, division (thus alienation), and correspondingly its salvation is constituted by the *unio-mystica*. The inner logic of such a structure necessarily implicates pantheism and an it-God. Mysticism generally and Jewish mysticism in particular are essentially characterized by the pantheistic it-God. But again, it is interesting to note how Jewish mysticism strives to accommodate itself to the normative view by mitigating the pantheism and the it-God implied in its structure. Aside from often using language that obscures and hides the implicated it-God and the pantheistic view, the mitigation impinges on the very substance of the mystical structure.

Jewish mysticism replaces the *unio-mystica* by the notion of *D'vekut*: that is, the gluing of the mystic to the Divine. *D'vekut* as the consummation of the mystic's striving brings the mystic as close and near to the Divine as possible and yet, most significantly, safeguards a distinction between the two. As such, the pantheistic oneness necessarily implicated by the *unio-mystica* is clearly mitigated towards a theistic dualism. And as regards the God-idea, there is no escaping the fact that the ultimate being, the *Ein-Sof* (the infinite) is an it-being. The *Ein-Sof* is perceived as the maximal, uncompromised expression of a being-in-itself and for-itself (the being-for-itself when encompassing the totality of manifested power in itself; i.e., when it is the pantheistic it-God, is perforce tantamount to being a being-in-itself). As such, it can only be an it-God (for while being-in-itself and for-itself are the forms of existence par excellence for the it-being, they are simply inapplicable to the Thou-being). It is significant, however, that Jewish mysticism, by and large, does not centre its speculative interest on the *Ein-Sof*; its speculation is directed to that realm of the Divine that constitutes the *sefirot*: i.e., emanations. Its interest is centred not on the notion of the Divine in itself, but on the Divine as it is related to the world. And here, in the realm of the *sefirot*, it introduces many of the Thou-God characterizations. Although the Divine as it is in itself is an it, the Divine with which Jewish mysticism mainly deals has many characterizations of the Thou.

But Jewish mysticism goes even further. It not only shifts its interest from one divine being to another, from the Divine-in-itself, the it-Godhead, to the Divine impinging on the world, the apparent Thou-God; it introduces characterizations of the Thou-God into the Divine-in-itself, the it-Godhead. Thus, the *sefirot* are placed ontologically within the *Ein-Sof* and in some formulations the act of *Zimzum*, the Divine contraction making room for its emanations, is seen not as a mechanical, blind act but as a free volitional act on the part of the *Ein-Sof* (indeed, some refer to the *Ein-Sof* as *Baal Ha-Razon*, the possessor of will). We have here a most intriguing attempt to combine an it-God with a Thou-God in one and the same being.

This intriguing attempt finds an even more striking and vivid expression in the phenomenon of Hasidism. In its speculative-theological superstructure Hasidism belongs to Jewish mysticism and thus the above mentioned speculative accommodations made by classical Jewish mysticism to mitigate the pantheistic it-God in the direction of the theistic Thou-God are essentially taken over by Hasidism. In the domain of abstract speculation Hasidism is not particularly innovative. Indeed, basically Hasidism is not interested in the realm of abstract speculation; its concern is not with God in himself. The genius and distinctive mark of Hasidism lie in its passionate, all-absorbing interest in the living encounter between God and man. It is involved with the God-for-man (i.e., the 'God for me') rather than with God in himself—with the revealing, communicating God rather than with the *Ein-Sof*. Hasidism is the conversion of mystical gnosis into ethos.

## A SYMBIOSIS OF THOU-GOD AND IT-GOD?

In this context the pull of the normative concept of a personal God is so much more vividly displayed. For in dealing with God in relation to man rather than with God in himself, any formulation within Judaism will find it extremely difficult not to deal with the Thou-God. Also, in this context the challenge is not so much to ascribe the characterizations of a Thou-God to an it-God in himself (though this does find a striking expression in the thought of the Maggid of Mezeritch) but rather to effect a combination of the Thou-God and the pantheistic view. And in Hasidism we witness the most striking expression in Judaism of just such a combination. Being ethos rather than gnosis, Hasidism is not so hampered by speculative and theoretical problems and complications and can, therefore, present a fiery religious affirmation of both the reality of the Thou-God and a view of pantheism.

Inasmuch as combining the Thou-God with pantheism is an intriguing challenge, an enticement to have the best of both possible worlds, we should carefully study the phenomenon of Hasidism. The pantheist view is very widespread and holds many enticements for the religious consciousness; Judaism, on the other hand, is the most dedicated and thoroughgoing instance of the Thou-God formulation with its serious challenge to the religious consciousness. As such, when the two are combined, as is the case in Jewish mysticism (particularly in Hasidism), we are presented with a most interesting phenomenon. However, whether such a symbiosis is, in the last analysis, possible, is a different matter.

## Bibliography

*Encyclopedia Judaica* (New York, 1971), 'value God', Vol. 7, pp. 641–74; 'value Hasidism' (Basic ideas and teachings of Hasidism), Vol. 7, pp. 1403–13.

Y. Kaufmann, *The Religion of Israel*, translated and abridged by M. Greenberg (Chicago, 1960), ch. 3, pp. 60–122; ch. 6, pp. 223–41; ch. 9, pp. 316–29.

J. Guttmann, *Philosophies of Judaism*, translated by D. Silverman (New York, 1964), ch. II, section 3 (neo-Platonism), pp. 84–133; section 4 (Aristotelianism), pp. 134–241; ch. III, section 2 (post-Kantian idealism), pp. 304–49.

E. Urbach, *Hazal* (The Sages) (Jerusalem, 1969), chs. 2, 3, 4 and 5, pp. 15–81; ch. 9, pp. 161–89; ch. 11, pp. 227–54.

G. F. Moore, *Judaism* (New York, 1971), part II, 'The Idea of God', pp. 357–444.

G. Scholem, *Kabbalah* (Jerusalem, 1974), ch. 3, pp. 87–116, 128–52.

———, *Major Trends in Jewish Mysticism* (New York, 1941), ch. 1, pp. 1–39; ch. 9, pp. 325–50.

L. Jacobs, *A Jewish Theology* (New York, 1973), chs. 2, 3 and 4, pp. 21–72; chs. 8 and 9, pp. 114–36; ch. 16, pp. 231–43.

I. Epstein, *Emunat Ha-Yahadut* (The Faith of Judaism) (Jerusalem, 1965), ch. 8, pp. 69–85.

M. Buber, *The Origin and Meaning of Hasidism*, translated by M. Friedman (New York, 1960), chs. 4, 5 and 6, pp. 113–200.

R. Schatz-Uffenheimer, *Ha-Hasidut Ke-Mistika* (Hasidism as Mysticism) (Jerusalem, 1968), chs. 1 and 2, pp. 21–31; chs. 7, 8 and 9, pp. 95–128.

Raniero Cantalamessa

# The Development of the Concept
# of a Personal God
# in Christian Spirituality

WE can distinguish two stages in the development of the Christian conception of a personal God: (*a*) an implicit stage in which the personal character of God is still expressed in terms of biblical monotheism; (*b*) an explicit stage characterised by the emergence of the problem of the Trinity and the introduction of the concept 'person'. It was a process by which faith in a personal God became faith in a God 'in three persons'.

## PERSONAL MONOTHEISM: THE BEGINNING

What I have called the first stage continues from certain points of view until the beginning of the third century. During this period the encounter with the religious philosophy of the Greeks forced Christians to realize the different, that is to say personal, nature of the biblical God, from the 'gods of the philosophers'. One indication of this is the refusal (absolute in the Septuagint with a single exception in the New Testament: Paul's speech on the Areopagus) to use the neuter form *to theion* to designate God. The difference is brought out particularly clearly when pagans and Christians (e.g., Justin and Celsus) discuss the relationship between God and the world, and God and history. The God of Plato—to whom man should aspire, but who cannot 'come down to men'[1]—and the God of Aristotle who 'moves by being loved'[2] (not by loving, and loving 'first') are for contemplation (*homoiosis theo*), not history. God in fact is conceived as an *object*, not as an active *subject* who acts on the world and converses with man. In other words, he is not thought of as a person.

To the need for a 'God who is near to take part in human affairs' (Maximus of Tyre), Hellenism offers two opposite answers. One is the Stoic nature-God, who is supreme but not personal (Cleanthes defines him as the "law and destiny of all things" and the bond of universal *sympatheia*). The other is the panoply of intermediate deities in all the religious systems of the time: 'personal divinities' who are not God in the true, supreme sense. A synthesis between the personal and the impersonal in God was sought for by distinguishing different levels of the divine being.

On the Christian side we see a series of processes in action which prepared the way for the personalism of the Trinity. One of these was the changing of God's appellations from the sphere of nature to the personal. 'Father' from 'father of the cosmos' (Plato) or 'Father of Israel' becomes 'Father of our Lord Jesus Christ' (Rom. 15:6). *Agennetos*, which for the Greeks meant the divine absolute (nature), becomes relational: i.e., the person of the Father—so much so that its opposite *gennetos* can also be used of God (cf. the 'genitus non factus' of Nicea). And, most significant of all, there is the personalization of 'Spiritus', which retains its ancient 'natural' meaning (spirit = force, viz. substance of God) and also acquires a new 'personal' one (Spirit = third divine person). Another process tending to bring out the personal in God is prosopographic exegesis, which points to the existence of an internal conversation within the divinity in certain passages of the Bible (such as Gen. 1:26: 'Faciamus hominem . . .' Ps. 110:1: 'Dixit Dominus Domino meo') and thus the presence of different divine speakers (*Gesprächspartner*) or 'persons' (in the sense of grammatical subjects).

### THE INTRODUCTION OF THE CONCEPT OF PERSON INTO THEOLOGY

The second stage in the development of the personal concept of God begins during the early years of the third century with the use of the concept *persona* in theology. Hippolitus speaks of the Father and the Son as 'two prosopa'.[3] Tertullian includes the Holy Spirit and speaks of 'tres personae'.[4] What meaning was given to the word *persona* by those who introduced it into theological language? Certainly neither the legal meaning of 'subject in law' (Harnack) nor the weak sense that could be derived from biblical expressions such as Proverbs 8:30 (*cotidie oblectabar in persona ipsius*), Lam. 4:20 and others where *persona* (the translation of *prosopon*) means face. This externalising sense occurred to none of the theologians, not even to Sabellius and the modalists for they always spoke of 'una persona' in God and made the rigid equation *unus Deus—unus Spiritus—una substantia—una persona.* Can we thus assume that the term 'person' had from the beginning the meaning of speaker in a conversation, or grammatical subject as in prosopographic exegesis?[5] In my opinion, prosopographic exegesis prepared the way for the use of the term *persona*, but only determined the sense in which it was used in a secondary manner. It brought out the plurality in God, perhaps it helped to make the term *persona* acceptable. But when the word *persona* was finally adopted by theology it appeared with a different sense, showing that it must have also had a different provenance. That was the sense which the word *prosopon* (and more frequently *persona*) had in the common secular usage of the time: individual, a particular human being, a particular member of a species: in this case, the human species.[6] *Persona* was a term that theology picked up, so to speak, in the street and it did not originally have any technical definition or philosophical genealogy. But as soon as it was adopted, its development began by its being set against *substantia*. This opposition *substantia-persona*[7] clearly demarcates its metaphysical setting. But in order to understand the original meaning of *persona* it is also essential to bear in mind the apposition *persona-res*. Tertullian calls the Son 'res et persona quaedam'; the Father and the Son are 'duae res unius substantiae', in which 'duae res' stands for 'duae personae'.[8] In this structure of usage the term *persona* is very close to *hypostasis*, in the sense this term acquired in theology (concrete object, tangible thing, as opposed to tenuous, unsolid).[9] Hence *hypostasis* is often used as an equivalent for *pragma*: i.e., *res*. The intention of calling the Word *persona* is to deny that he is merely 'flatus vocis', 'breath of the voice', or something insubstantial, as the Modalists claimed.[10] *Persona* originally meant individuality and objectivity; or, rather, an objective individuality.

In this sense, the word spread peacefully throughout the Latin world, until the fourth century when a major crisis arose. But before I talk about that, I must take a brief look at the parallel process which had led Greek theology to formulate the personal in God with the term *hypostasis*. Origen was the first to use the formula 'three hypostases' to designate the Father, the Son and the Holy Spirit.[11] The sense was the one I have already mentioned: a concrete and objective reality, a distinct individual within a species: something, therefore, formally distinct from *ousia*. This formula of Origen's had the misfortune of being later used by the Arians and was thus condemned by the Council of Nicea, which affirmed, by anathema, that *hypostasis* and *ousia* were perfectly synonymous. The Cappadocians, in particular St Basil of Caesarea, rescued Greek theology from the blind alley this had led it into. He defined the distinction between *ousia* and *hypostasis* in God: 'Between *ousia* and *hypostasis* there is the same difference as that between the common and the particular (*to kath'ekaston*), between living being and a particular man'.[12] The problem with this language is that it seems still to distinguish the essential and the personal in God as genus and species, or species and individuals. But the important point was reached: the personal or rather tri-personal character of the biblical God was reformulated in the trinitarian context and not at a level below that of the divine being (as Arius, extreme defender of the Greek way, had proposed), but at the same level as the impersonal: that is to say, in full and absolute consubstantiality. From this point of view, the Nicean *homoousios* marks the parting of the ways between Hellenism and Christianity.

The Latin trinitarian formula ('one substance in three persons') and the Greek ('one *ousia* in three *hypostases*') came into conflict at Antioch, where there were two opposed communities: the Melezian supported by the Cappadocians and the Pauline supported by the Latins and Alexandrians. The dispute broke out because the Latins tried to impose the formula *tria prosopa* (corresponding to *tres personae*) on the Greeks. Each side attacked the terminology of the other; the Greeks criticized *prosopon* (*persona*) and the Latins *hypostasis*. The latter could not accept *hypostasis* because they regarded it as synonymous with *substantia*, and were unaware of the individual sense in which it was used by the Cappadocians in the wake of Origen.[13] But why were the Greeks so critical of the term *persona*? Their criticism was based on a linguistic mistake, which in spite of frequent denials (most recently by Prestige) continues to be perpetrated from manual to manual: viz., the presumed Modalist origin of *persona*. St Basil of Caesarea circulated this view in several of his letters, according to which Sabellius said that God is a single *hypostasis* represented in Scripture as various *personae*: viz., under various guises, in accordance with the aspect (*prosopon*) he assumed to manifest himself to mankind.[14]

But, in spite of these difficulties, agreement was reached between Latins and Greeks before too long through a compromise by which the Latins recognised the orthodoxy of the term *hypostasis* and the Greeks that of *persona*. The chief creator of the reconciliation was St Gregory of Nazianzen, who succeeded at the ecumenical council of Constantinople (381) in having a theological equivalence accepted between the formula 'three *hypostases*' and the formula 'three *personae*'.[15]

### PERSONAL-IMPERSONAL AND SUBJECTIVE-OBJECTIVE IN GOD

Towards the end of the fourth century, the second stage of the transformation of biblical personal monotheism into trinitarian monotheism was concluded. This stage was characterized by the use of the concept *persona*. It apparently ended with total agreement between Greek and Latin theology. 'Is it possible to conceive,' exclaimed St Gregory of Nazianzen, 'of a fuller agreement or to express more absolutely the same thing, even though in diferent words?'[16] But modern dogmatic historians have raised various doubts about the reality of this agreement. Were the Greeks and the Latins really saying the same thing in different words?

De Regnon points out the primary difference between them. In considering the Trinity, Greeks and Latins approached it from different aspects. The Greeks started with the divine persons (i.e., plurality), and thence arrived at the divine nature and unity. The Latins, on the other hand, started from the divine nature or unity, and thence arrived at the persons. 'The Latin considers personality as a mode of nature; the Greek considers nature as the content of person.'[17] There is some truth in this, which might perhaps be confirmed by analysing the distinctive character of eastern as compared with western spirituality and mysticism. The Latin mystic usually converses with 'God' or 'Jesus Christ'. Only rarely is the trinitarian schema 'to the Father, through the Son, in the Holy Spirit' his primary approach. It is a mysticism centred on the divine in general, even though there are many varieties and exceptions to be taken into account. (For example, St Teresa of Avila describes one of her visions of the Trinity as there being 'three distinct persons, who can be talked to separately'[18]: i.e., three speakers.)

Although there is some truth in de Regnon's thesis, the way it has been used in apologetics makes it now appear misleading in several ways. I think it is more precise to say that both Greeks and Latins start from God's unity (the Greek and the Latin creeds begin: 'Credo in unum Deum'). But this unity is conceived by the Latins as impersonal or pre-personal: it is God's essence which then becomes specified as Father, Son and Holy Spirit (although of course this essence is not thought of as pre-existing the persons). The Greeks on the other hand conceive of an already personalized unity, because 'the unity is the Father, from whom and towards whom proceed the other persons'.[19] The first article of their creed is 'Credo in unum Deum Patrem omnipotentem', in which 'Patrem omnipotentem' is not detached from 'unum Deum', as in the Latin creed. This is the precise point the Latins contest, seeing in it an incipient subordinationism. 'The name "God"', writes Augustine, 'indicates the whole Trinity, not just the Father.'[20] If we wanted a formula to express this difference, we could say that for the Latins God is 'unum in Trinitate' (in fact, this is the formula in the Athanasian creed), whereas for the Greeks he is 'unus in Trinitate'. For the Latins, God is the divine essence; for the Greeks, the person of the Father.

Schmaus and others[21] have criticized the Latin Augustinian conception of God for giving the supreme position in its divine system to the impersonal God of the philosophers: the One of Plotinus, instead of the biblical God. But, apart from the fact that this danger is not exclusive to Latin theology (what about Pseudo-Denis?), I do not think it is useful to make such a criticism without mentioning the opposite danger of subordinationism and even tritheism present in the Greek view. The conclusion to be drawn is that neither view on its own is sufficient to establish firmly the integrity of the faith. The mystery is at the centre, not to one side or the other. It lies in the synthesis and balance between unity and plurality, the impersonal and the personal. But the fact that there are two ways is a gain for theology, not an embarrassment to be overcome. Ecumenism between Orthodoxy and Roman Catholicism expresses a deeply felt need in both theologies.

A second doubt about the fourth-century agreement is that raised by Prestige: Is it true that the Latin *persona* and the Greek *hypostasis* are saying the same thing about the Trinity, as Gregory of Nazianzen maintained in all good faith? Prestige says No. *Persona* implies the idea of *subject, hypostasis* of object: 'For the Greeks God is a single objective being, although he is also three objects . . .; for the Latins God is a single object and three subjects'.[22] If that is right, it means that it is only possible in Latin theology to speak of divine personalism in the modern sense, or of subjectivity in God. This would mean that the Greek view is tied to a fundamentally Platonic conception of the Deity (divinity as an object of contemplation rather than an active subject).

This thesis also contains a valid insight. In its favour we could point out that *persona* appears to have absorbed the idea of 'speaker' from prosopographic exegesis, which is absent from the concept *hypostasis*. There is also the point that only *persona* is used specifically of a rational being (every person is also an *hypostasis* but not every *hypostasis* is a person). If both *persona* and *hypostasis* are used in theology to mean 'an objective individuality', it is also true that *persona* lays more stress on the individuality and *hypostasis* on the objectivity.

However, Prestige's view would be fundamentally false if it suggested that the Latin use of *persona* involved the idea of subject in the modern sense of the term, which implies self-consciousness (the 'ego'). Indeed, that sense of the term was unknown to antiquity and not introduced into theology until the advent of idealism (Günther). For the Fathers, *persona* connotes the substance (*res, pragma*) and not the self-reflective consciousness of Kant. From this point of view, the personalism of classical theology has very little in common with modern subjectivism. Even Augustine, who uses the psychological analogy, writes: 'When we speak of the person of the Father, we mean simply the substance of the

Father.'[23] That means that if we apply the term person to the Trinity in the de-ontologized sense of 'consciousness', the relation between the personal and the impersonal, the plurality and unity in God, are the reverse of those intended by the ancient formulations.

In the language of the Fathers 'one substance in three persons' means that God is one subject (= one consciousness, one will, one freedom, one love) in three distinct objectivities, or individuations. Using the terms in the idealist or modern sense, the same formula would mean that God is one single object (nature) in three subjects or three distinct 'egos'. When Bulgakov proposes that we speak of the Trinity as 'one person in three hypostases'[24] he is making an attempt—questionable but interesting—to change the words in order not to change the meaning. Indeed, given the new semantic content of the term 'person', the ancient formula only retains its meaning if it is adapted in this way (of course, another solution would be to dispute the new psychological content of the term 'person', or to ignore it in theology).

## DOGMATIC AND THEOLOGICAL VALUE OF PERSON

Augustine expressed an extremely pessimistic view on the usefulness of both the term *persona* and the term *hypostasis*. He said that in speaking of the Trinity their usefulness was reducible to the fact that they enabled us to say something and not say nothing at all when we are asked what the 'three' are.[25] If we consider how the term *persona* was introduced into theology, we must admit that Augustine was right: the term arose from the need to find a single word for the Father, the Son and the Holy Spirit which would avoid having constantly to repeat the number 'tres' or the 'nomina'. *Persona* has a pronominal value: it stands instead of the noun or name; it does not predicate anything. Among the Greeks, St Gregory of Nazianzen seems to wish to show on several occasions that the trinitarian dogma can be proclaimed perfectly correctly by doing without either the term *hypostasis* or the term *persona*.[26] He seems to be saying that God is both *one* and *three*: that is the faith. Saying that God is one nature and three persons is merely one way of putting it.

The problem arises of the dogmatic or normative value of the term *persona* in trinitarian theology. In my opinion, it is very small, whereas in Christology it is an integral part of the Chalcedonian definition. No council promulgated its use in trinitarian theology, and I do not think that its use in the *Tomus Damasi* (DB 173) is a sufficient basis upon which to establish its dogmatic value. Of course, it is the term constantly used by tradition from a certain period onwards. But tradition itself declares the optional and provisional nature of the term. The concept *persona* crept into theology, was allowed to stay (with many reservations), and finally came to be considered an essential part of faith in the Trinity.

But its theological value is more solid. *Persona* (and *hypostasis*), of all the philosophical concepts taken over from secular language, best expresses the originality of Christianity. Its very invention (insofar as it was conceived of as distinct from the Aristotelian prime substance) was a work of theology: Christian reflection on God (and successively on Jesus Christ) forced it to go beyond the confines of Greek metaphysics, and to produce from the 'naturalism' of antiquity the reality of the person which St Thomas rightly defines as 'that which most perfectly exists of all that is real'.[27] But that point was only reached slowly and laboriously. As we have seen it did not have such likely beginnings. It was much easier to talk about the divine nature (that is, the divine impersonal), than about the divine persons (which represented what was philosophically unexpected in the faith). But many of the difficulties arose from the persistence of the initial empirical significance of *persona*. We might say that its metaphysical journey began with Boethius and that the first stage ended with Aquinas.

In many respects, the thought of Aquinas was a milestone in the development of the concept of person. I mention only those points which supplement the Fathers' thinking. He distinguished and clarified the difference between *persona* and *hypostasis* and definitively recognized the concrete rather than abstract character of *hypostasis*, as used in Greek theology. He accepted Rusticus' correction of Boethius' definition and translated *hypostasis* by *subsistentia*, meaning 'id quod per se existit et non in alio': i.e., that which exists of itself and not in another'.[28] Secondly, he sorted out many ambivalences by distinguishing the provenance of the term *persona* from its destination: in the former, it was not correctly applied to God; in the latter, it applied to God 'in modo summo'.[29] But what is the theological meaning assumed by *persona* in trinitarian usage? St Thomas replies in one of the most closely argued articles of the *Summa*: it is the 'relatio ut subsistens': the subsistent relationship[30]—a definition which Aquinas has taken from the whole Latin tradition, and primarily Augustine. It is impossible to analyze this definition here. I want only to point out how it resolves many traditional difficulties and completes a whole process of dogmatic clarification. Nature and person are distinguished in God as absolute and relative, but now it is clearly and definitively stated that the relative in God is also absolute (*subsistens*). Impersonal and personal are at the same level of the divine being and not on two different metaphysical planes, as with the Greeks and also in other religions (for example, Hinduism recognizes below the impersonal divine, the Brahman, a whole descending series of divine personifications. There is another advantage to be noted in the Thomistic definition. It opened the theological concept of person to the idea of the inter-personal: the *I*-thou (the word *persona* came into theology in the plural and was never used of God in the singular). That is the dimension that some modern linguistic analysis stresses in the concept of person: its being 'ad alios'.[31] St Thomas certainly boosted this idea by defining person as a subsistent relationship.

## CONCLUSION

Simone Weil has written that we cannot admit the Christian Trinity without conceiving of God as both impersonal and personal at one and the same time.[32] This judgment (which originally had a negative intention) acquires an important methodological significance in the context of a reinterpretation of the personal and impersonal in God. Surely the Trinity is the point of balance and synthesis between these two irreducible aspects of any authentic conception of God which would maintain his transcendence *and* his relevance to mankind? That, at any rate, is what I have tried to show in this historical reconstruction. If we leave that out of any discussion of the 'personal God' we fall into the danger often held against Latin theology: thinking of God 'etsi Trinitas non daretur'; as if the Trinity did not exist.

*Translated by Dinah Livingstone*

## Notes

1. Plato, *Symposium* 203a.
2. Aristotle, *Metaphysics* 7, 1072, b3.
3. *C. Noetum* 7, 14.
4. *Adv. Praxean* 12, 3; for Tertullian see my study: *La cristologia di Tertulliano* (Paradosis 18) (Fribourg, 1962), pp. 159ff.
5. Cf. C. Andressen, 'Zur Entstehung und Geschichte des trinitarischen Personbegriffes', in *Zeitschrift neut. Wiss.* 52 (1961), pp. 1–39.
6. Cf. M. Nédoncelle, 'Prosopon et persona dans l'antiquité classique', in *Rev. sc. rel.* 22 (1948), pp. 298ff.
7. *Adv. Praxean* 12, 6; 15, 1 ('distinctio personalis'); *Adv. Valentinianos* 7, 3 ('substantialiter-personaliter').
8. *Adv. Praxean* 7, 5; 13, 10.
9. Cf. G. Prestige, *God in Patristic Thought* (London, 1952).

10. *Adv. Praxean* 7, 5.

11. Cf. *C. Celsum* VIII, 12; *In Joh. Evang.* II, 10, 75.

12. *Ep.* 136, 6; cf. also *Ep.* 38 (by Gregory of Nyssa?) *Ep.* 214.

13. Cf. St Jerome, *Ep.* 15, 3, 4 (PL 22, 356).

14. Cf. *Ep.* 214, 3; 226, 4.

15. Cf. *Or.* 21, 35; 42, 16; (PG 35, 1124; 36, 476).

16. *Ibid.* 42, 16 (PG 36, 477).

17. T. de Renon, *Etudes de théologie positive sur la Sainte Trinité*, Vol. I (Paris, 1892), p. 433.

18. *Spiritual Relation* XXXIII (Avila, 1572).

19. Gregory Naz., *Or.* 42, 15 (PG 36, 476B).

20. *Trin.* I, 6, 10; cf. also IX, 1, 1 ('credamus Patrem et Filium et Spiritum Sanctum esse unum Deum').

21. Cf. M. Schmaus, 'Die Spannung von Metaphysik und Heilsgeschichte in der Trinitätslehre Augustins', in *Studia Patr.* 6 (=TU 81) (Berlin, 1962), p. 504; V. Lossky, *Théologie mystique de l'Eglise d'Orient* (Paris, 1944).

22. Prestige, *op. cit.*, p. 245.

23. *Trin.* VII, 6, 11.

24. P. Bulgakov, *Du Verbe incarne* (Paris, 1943), pp. 13ff.

25. *Trin.* VII, 6, 11.

26. Cf. *Or.*, 23, 8 (PG 35, 1160); 42, 16 (PG 36, 477).

27. St Thomas, *S. Th.*, I, 29, 1.

28. *Ibid.* I, 29, 2.

29. *Ibid.* I, 29, 3, ad. 2.

30. *Ibid.* I, 29, 4.

31. Cf. E. Schillebeeckx, *Jesus, het verhaal van een levende* (Bloemendaal, 1974).

32. S. Weil, *Lettre à un religieux* (Paris, 1951), p. 36.

# PART III

*Recent Theological Reflection*

Jan Peters

# Naming the Unnameable

MODERN parents frequently give their children names that shock the grandparents. It is, of course, possible to make light of the shock caused by saying nonchalantly: 'What's in a name?'. In that case, this article will arouse little interest, since it is exclusively concerned with giving a name to God in our culture. I shall not consider the problem of God's existence at all. All that will be discussed here is the human act of giving the essentially unnameable reality known in the western tradition as God a name.

The shock felt by grandparents about the names that are so often given to their grandchildren may be well-founded, since they perhaps recognize intuitively that there is much more to giving a name than simply a desire to provide a practical means of distinguishing people from each other. The grandparents cannot find in many of these new names the scarlet thread that runs through the generations. They are only aware of a break with earlier generations in many of these foreign-sounding names.

Something very similar is happening in the sphere of religion today: many strange and unfamiliar names are occurring in the language of religion for God. To take one example, Huub Oosterhuis[1] gives new names to God in each of his publications. It is possible to call his names poetical, since he is not a theologian, but, quite apart from the fact that theologians were originally also poets, theologians are bound to ask what kind of experience of faith is to be found in this phenomenon of giving (or not giving) names to God.

Generally speaking, we can say that, in giving a name, man is expressing understanding; he is making a distinction and he is accepting something into the totality of his conscious existence. Giving a name has something to do with the relationship between the one who gives and the one who is given the name.[2] It is not a matter of indifference whether I call someone by his Christian name or by his surname. It is also theologically significant that the period that followed the 'God is dead' theology began with a renewed search for a name for the unnameable. The arguments used by the theologians of this movement were also so devoid of feeling that one could look in vain for any expression of sadness or mourning in the very significant statement that God was dead.

This comment is not intended to criticize a movement that now belongs to the past. On the contrary, it is to draw attention to the importance of feeling in the giving of names, which belongs to the affective level in man and expresses a human longing.

My first point in this article is an attempt to support this claim. This will be followed by an intermediate observation to the effect that, despite the fact that the name 'Jesus' definitively expresses God and his concern with humanity, theology can never be reduced to Christology. My second point is this: it is essential for theology that God should be named again and again in any living culture, whether this is done in order to deny his existence or to praise him in a new way. Finally, I shall make a number of observations about the political consequences of giving God names. In this respect, Christianity is essentially different from those religions in which God is not experienced personally and which recoil from the inner dynamism of naming him and from recognizing him as the God who makes man's history a history of salvation.

In these final observations, I shall rely to a great extent on my knowledge of St John of the Cross and on my experience of contemporary religious movements that claim to make eastern mysticism accessible to western man.

### LONGING AS A SOURCE OF GIVING NAMES

In some modern publications on the subject of giving names to God[3] one is conscious that the authors cling so stubbornly to names that have already been given in the past that they want apparently to put up barriers against the longing that has its origin in a vital faith to give a new name or new names to the essentially intangible ultimate reality that is God. New names are, however, given, as we have seen at the beginning of this article. The theologian can, moreover, never regard himself as exonerated from the task of looking for the causes of such phenomena.

Let me begin by saying that giving a name to God is not so much a question of defining the concept of God so that his incomprehensibility will cease to exist, as of accepting a challenge that originates from God's concealment.[4] This distinction between God's incomprehensibility and his concealment may at first sight seem to be a fine academic point which has little connexion with real life. On closer examination, however, we shall see that his incomprehensibility is an affirmation at the noetic level, whereas his concealment is a challenge at the affective level. Mystics have always been more intrigued by God's concealment than by his incomprehensibility. 'Where are you hidden, Beloved . . .? I ran and called after you and you had disappeared without a trace'— these words at the beginning of St John of the Cross' *Spiritual Canticle* are full of affective terms and free of all noetic concern. This makes us suspect that it is meaningful to call out a name in this context of concealment.

Religiousness comes about whenever longing and God's concealment come together in correlation and do not cancel each other out. Christian faith in God's revelation of himself does not do away with God's concealment or with the longing. The revealed God continues to be a concealed God and the latter also arouses longing.

There is clearly a difference here between the Judaeo-Christian religion and eastern religions such as Buddhism. According to Buddhist teaching, the highest form of perfection is to be found in the death of longing. Many longings are, however, expressed in the Bible. All the longings of biblical man are rooted in his desire and need to share the fulness of life by means of a total unfolding of his being. The words of Jesus Ben Sirach: 'Do not deny yourself the good day and do not let the part of a good desire escape you' (Ecclus. 14:14) may not be an expression of the supreme wisdom of the Bible, but they do show that longing or desire was normal to biblical man. In the New Testament, this longing is purified: men shall 'have life and have it abundantly' (John 10:10).

Scripture gives full recognition to the natural presence and positive value of longing. There is no suggestion in the Bible that longings should be killed—they are to be purified and raised up. There are many examples of this: 'As a hart longs for flowing streams' (Ps. 42:1); 'As the eyes of servants look to the hand of their master . . .' (Ps. 123:2); 'My soul waits (=longs) for the Lord more than the watchmen for the morning' (Ps. 130:6); 'Fill me with joy and gladness' (Ps. 51:10). Even the old man whom God has 'made to see so many sore troubles' must not let go of hope, for God will 'revive me again . . . and will bring me up again' (Ps. 71:20ff).

Scripture is full of man's intense longing for God. There is a deep longing behind the desire to possess wisdom (Prov. 8:19; Ecclus. 1:20), nostalgia for Jerusalem (Ps. 137:5), the wish to go up to the Temple (Ps. 121:1), the desire to know the word of God in all its forms (Ps. 119:20, 131) and so on.

All the thrust of this longing is directed towards God and to achieve this end all illusions and imitations have to be laid bare (Amos 5:18; Isa. 58:2) and all disappointment has to be overcome: 'There is nothing upon this earth that I desire besides thee. My flesh and my heart may fail, but God is the strength of my heart and my portion for ever . . . For me it is good to be near God . . . May I tell of his works' (Ps. 73: 25–26, 28; cf. 42:2; 63:1).

In Jesus this longing is passionate: 'I have earnestly desired to eat this passover with you' (Luke 22:15). At the very end of the Book of Revelation, the Spirit and the Bride express a cry of longing: 'Come!' (Rev. 22:17).

In this context, it is interesting to note the attitude taken by Freud and his followers towards the question of longing or desire. Freud observed that the objects of many of his patients' longings were illusory. One of these illusory objects of desire was, in Freud's opinion, God. It should not, however, be forgotten that Freud was in contact with sick people and that the pathological pattern that he found in his patients was not the normal one.

Nabert (*Le désir de Dieu*), Pohier, Vergote and especially Ricoeur[5] have been less suspicious of human longing. Ricoeur has made a clear distinction between illusory and non-illusory longing, but longing as such he regards as man's basic dynamism. To simplify very radically what he has said on this subject, Ricoeur has distinguished a longing that is enclosed within itself and looks back in search of something in the past that may satisfy it and another type of longing that is directed outwards and forward. Longing can also be distinguished from a consumptive wish by the fact that it can never be fulfilled. According to Ricoeur, the subject has to accept that his longing is incapable of fulfilment. The gospel message of God, who is concerned with man, can take this longing away from itself and transform it. Longing has to be corrected, moreover, by an offer from outside so that it cannot run after itself. Ricoeur believed that there was only one way of escaping from a longing that is thrown back on itself and that was by accepting new impulses from elsewhere.

Longing can, however, neither be corrected nor can it break out of the illusory circle of itself by means of words, images or figures arising from the subject. This correction or breaking out has to come from outside, that is, from what is 'strange'. It would, of course, take far more than this article to show that what comes to the longing subject from Scripture is not the selfish longing of the subject himself. There is a danger here if Scripture is regarded as the Word of God which has been recorded once and for all and requires no further exegesis. The dynamic power of revelation continues in every conscious believer. One of the ways in which the 'strange' element comes to the longing subject is in the challenge of the mystery of the concealed God.

I have already said that God's concealment should not be regarded naively as a concealment that will ever be cancelled out. God will continue to be a concealed God. And the strangeness also remains, demanding that the longing subject should above all call and venture into the invocative sphere of words: in other words, to call a name. Not to conjure up the strange element, but to take the longing self out of itself and to transcend longing. The longing subject is in this way estranged from itself and transformed. It is no longer exclusively concerned with itself. It risks a call, directed outwards.

Ricoeur correctly attached great importance to language, especially the language of faith, Scripture, theology and spiritual dialogue, since this takes the longing subject out of itself and invites it to risk what may be called the betrayal of words and names. The longing subject risks a name for the unnameable and at the same time recoils from the name, because the reality that is hoped for is not and never will be covered by a name. At the same time, the longing subject remains alert, so that the name may not become an idol and that the longing may be satisfied with nothing less than God himself. This movement of longing is not in any sense a passive merging into a primordial ground, a *nirvana* or a vague pantheism.

I believe that the affirmation that God is a 'person' derives an entirely new content from this movement that I have outlined above. The God who is longed for in this sense estranges man from himself, but at the same time gives him back to himself in a new way. Ricoeur indicates this process by using the word 'dramatic'—something happens, longing is transformed and what is longed for is also transformed. The longing that simply feels at one with the cosmos seems to me to be a pathetic longing that prevents man from being man and, in the Christian sense, also prevents God from being man. The 'concealed' God of Christianity (and Judaism) is, in Buddhism, for example, a 'salvaging' God, an oceanic deity. The process of becoming one, discussed by such Christian mystics as St John of the Cross, is a becoming one in estrangement. ('Everyone said: she is lost; but I had been found'.) Yet God continues to be the centre of the soul. Being faithful to myself may mean being faithful to God. 'Faithful' is used here in the sense of *fides*, faith or belief in the sense of believing someone (*credere alicui*). I cannot, however, leave that 'someone' nameless, just as Jesus of Nazareth did not leave the one to whom he was ultimately and deeply faithful nameless, but called him 'Father'. In the knowledge that this name 'Father' has given rise to all kinds of difficulties and new problems since Freud and as these problems are discussed elsewhere in the present number of *Concilium*, I shall not go into them here. I will simply go on to make a number of observations concerning the question as to whether the Christian who wants to reflect about the name of God nowadays can be satisfied by simply taking over this name second-hand.

### A NUMBER OF OBSERVATIONS

If we look back now at the theological publications that followed the 'death-of-God' theology some years ago, what is most striking is that the majority of the theologians who contributed to this debate concentrated their attention not so much on God as on Jesus of Nazareth. Theologians, in other words, became Christologians.[6] Some of these authors, Dorothee Sölle,[7] for example, and Bloch, went so far as to say that if Jesus Christ were alive today, he would be an atheist. In these writings, it was not really the *deus absconditus*, the concealed God, who was being discussed, but *homo absconditus*, the concealed man. In Scripture, Bloch encountered man. According to him, the concealed God had to be understood simply as an indication pointing in the direction of the concealed man. The theme of concealment in the history of mankind is, in Bloch's opinion, the gradual revelation of the *homo absconditus*, the making public of man's definitive and as yet unrealized humanity on earth. The 'divine' God must become a 'human' man. Faith in God will therefore gradually disappear as the human aspect penetrates increasingly into the idea of God and as man increasingly gives himself a place in the religious mystery.

The Christian theologian who believes in the mystery of God's becoming man should never regard God and man as in competition with each other. If he in fact allows one of the components of the paradox of the incarnation (man and God) to fall, he will at the same time be cancelling out that paradox. Again, if he looks exclusively for the utility or functionality of God in this way, he will also be depriving theology of its distinctiveness. For Bloch, the task of Christianity is to give depth to Marxism and to prevent it from sinking into a vulgar form of atheism.

One of the greatest merits of Schillebeeckx's recent book on Jesus is that, among other things, he points out that Jesus has no importance from the theological point of view if he is no more than one of us or no more than an addition to the long list of idealists who have failed from the human point of view. God was more central to Jesus of Nazareth than to anyone else. Schillebeeckx shows that, however interested in and sympathetic we may be today towards Jesus of Nazareth, we should not allow this at the expense of the God whom Jesus called Father. As theologizing about Jesus becomes a real discussion about

God, it at the same time becomes clear that there is an essential difference between the 'impersonal' God of such religions as Buddhism and
the 'personal' God of Jesus.

Erich Fromm[8] has pointed to a higher synthesis between Christianity
and those religions in which God is seen to be impersonal, but insists
that this synthesis can only be made possible if the mystery of the
incarnation is eliminated from Christian teaching. This is, for Fromm,
the central question. Is religious experience necessarily connected, he
asks, with a theological concept? He thinks not, since a religious experience can be described as a human experience (as though it were possible to speak of other experiences than human ones!). This human
experience is what forms the common basis for certain kinds of theistic
as well as non-theistic and atheistic conceptions. According to Fromm,
what makes the difference is not the substrate of experience that underlies the different conceptions, but the conception of the experience
itself. This type of experience is most clearly revealed in the mysticism
of Christianity, Islam and Judaism as well as in that of Zen Buddhism.
Fromm's conclusion is that if the experience itself rather than the conception is analyzed, it becomes clear that it is possible to speak of a
theistic and of a non-theistic religious experience.

It really depends on what is called 'religious'. Even if we do not
believe in a history of salvation pointing essentially to the future within
the history of mankind as such, we can accept that the longing or desire
referred to above in the context of our outline of Ricoeur's teaching[9]
can assume cosmic dimensions and this can be called religious. The
same applies, however, to the experience of a drug trip. In the Christian sense, 'religious' is applicable to the longing that is concerned with
a personal God who is mindful of man and shows this attitude within
human history.

Having said this, I would now like to turn to my own conception of
spirituality. There is a sharp contrast between two types of spirituality
today. These can be called the 'imitative' and the 'creative' forms of
spirituality. According to the first of these, spirituality is simply an *imitatio Christi* in the limited sense or possibly an *imitatio Dei* (Fromm).
The other form is a persistence of the incarnation of God in miniature,
as it were, in each human being, with the result that God is in this way
creatively active in the world.

I would opt for the second conception of spirituality. It is admittedly
an option, but it is firmly based on the teaching of St John of the
Cross. This brings me to the final part of my argument, namely that it
is only possible to give a name to the nameless God, who is also essentially unnameable, in prayer. In other words, giving a name to God is
the outcome of an association with faith and the content of faith in
longing.

### NAMING GOD AGAIN AND AGAIN FROM OUR OWN CULTURE

I will try in this section of my article to outline the way in which religious man's first movement towards naming God again begins with his longing and a longing that also becomes estranged from itself (a salutary estrangement) and is thus transformed. The estrangement comes about through Scripture, with its message of salvation for the world. Anyone who examines the message of redemption seriously finds himself faced with certain boundaries: 'I cannot! We cannot!' Wish and longing can be distinguished here—the wish is situated in the consumptive sphere and can be fulfilled, whereas longing is situated in the dynamic sphere and, although it cannot be fulfilled, it can be sustained. An encounter with this fundamental limitation is always accompanied by a longing to go beyond the boundary. This leads to an invocative call directed outwards.

Whenever Jesus encountered inhumanity, suffering, poverty and isolation, he found a new name for God who was concerned with man. This experience can be described in the following way—he became aware of who was protesting so effectively in him against poverty, isolation and so on that he was bold enough to say that the kingdom of God was at hand. Giving a name to God comes from the answer given in faith to the question: Who in me (or in us) is protesting now against evil? Is it perhaps a fashionable whim or a camouflaged instinct for self-preservation? Or is it really the concealed God?[10]

On the other hand, that God-in-me is so intricately involved in my life-history that a special story can be told. This is not necessarily a connected story. It may be a series of short stories, the main character in which is not a little independent person, but a man with a task, someone who is sent. In these stories, the unnameable is named again and again, perhaps even with bizarre names such as: nothing, strange island, night, formless, poor and so on. Each time, however, the unnameable appears recognizably as the main character.

In prayer, man discovers that it is God who is protesting in him (in the centre of his soul, as St John of the Cross would say or in the smallest unknown, as Oosterhuis would call it) effectively against the evil (isolation, discrimination, deprival of rights and so on) that occurs in my life.[11] When I say that man can in prayer again and again give new names that are connected with his culture, prayer must be understood in the momentous sense to which I have referred previously. That is, an association in longing with faith and the content of faith (see also *Concilium* 5, 1970, No. 2). Believing consciously means that throughout our lives we conjugate the verb 'to believe' not only in the indicative or the imperative, but also in the optative—the mood of longing. This is more than a grammatical joke, since man is his language and believing man is also his language. Do we not find the same language game in Scripture? Broadly speaking, it is possible to say that the historical books of the Old Testament are in the indicative, the Pentateuch, on the other hand, being in the imperative. There are, however, other books in the Old Testament and the Psalms, for example, repeat in the mood of longing what is contained in the historical books as information in the indicative and in the books of the Law as tasks in the imperative mood.

The same applies also to the New Testament—the accounts are in the indicative, the Sermon on the Mount is a classical example of the imperative and the Our Father is clearly in the optative. This model of prayer was called by the Fathers of the Church a *Breviarium totius Evangelii*. By this they meant a summary of the gospel written, not in the indicative mood of an account or story or in the imperative of the new law of Christ, but in the mood of longing, I am doing no more than indicate possibilities here, since it would take too long to show precisely how and where new names for God emerge again and again and the concealment of God is repeatedly stressed in those parts of Scripture that are written predominantly in the optative mood of longing.

Two elements occur again and again in the context of giving a name to God in the writings of St John of the Cross. Firstly, the God whom I want to name is present with me and with every man, but there is not always an affective presence nor is there always a transformed longing. Secondly, the name given to God is never the result of a revelation and no one should ever seek such a revelation.[12] 'He has given us his Son, his only Word', St John of the Cross declared, 'He has no other. In this one Word he has said everything. He has no more to say. If you want more, you can at the most expect such an answer as: "I have already told you everything in my Word . . . As for me, you should find nothing of revelations or visions which you can ask me or demand of me. As for you, look at him!"'

Saint John of the Cross undoubtedly found in himself—in the centre of his soul—new names. An example of such a name is: 'An I-do-not-know-what of which I can only stammer'. Sometimes he lets this 'what' extend itself into a whole string of images: 'wind breathing gently, the singing of nightingales, the magic of the forest and the flame that burns but does not hurt'.

It will be observed that the author does not simply use second-hand names[13] and this is clearly because such a practice would distort and do an injustice to the relationship with the one named.[14]

Let me conclude by asking this question: Is it really so important to give new names to God? The only possible answer is, whether it is important or not, it happens and this must make theologians think. It also seems to me to be the correct path to follow if we are to express God in a careful and warm way (especially since the death-of-God theology) and if we are to speak of God out of our own affective experience. It is also more honest than remaining silent about God or seeking refuge in an incomplete Christology. It may be no more than a beginning, an attempt to give a name to the unnameable, but it may initiate a renewed discourse on the subject of God. If our aim is to insist on the fact that Christianity is a historical religion then we must let it make history and not simply tell us about the past. If we do not do this, we shall be forced to keep silent, especially about the history of *salvation*. Giving a name to the unnameable has a past and a present. I hope that it will also have a future.

*Translated by David Smith*

## Notes

1. I have chosen Huub Oosterhuis out of many authors because most of his works have been translated into many of the languages of the readers of *Concilium*. His first and best known work is *Your Word is Near* (New York, 1968), which contains many examples of new names for God.

2. *Bibel-Lexikon* (Einsiedeln, Zürich and Cologne, 2nd edn., 1968), col. 1216–17, under 'Name Gottes'.

3. A good example is Maurice Clavel, *Dieu est Dieu, nom de Dieu* (Paris, 1976).

4. Karl Rahner, 'Über die Verborgenheit Gottes', in *Schriften zur Theologie* XII (Einsiedeln, Zürich and Cologne, 1975), pp. 285–305; the available books and articles are listed on p. 285, note 2.

5. Paul Ricoeur, 'L'image de Dieu et l'épopée humaine', in *Christianisme social* 68 (1960), pp. 493–514.

6. Heinz Zahrnt, *Wozu ist das Christentum gut?* (Munich, 1972).

7. Dorothee Sölle, *Das Recht ein anderer zu werden* (Hamburg, 1971), p. 57.

8. Erich Fromm, *You Shall be as Gods* (New York, 1966), especially chapter 2 on the concept of God.

9. Paul Ricoeur, 'Icône et image', in *La métaphore vive* (Paris, 1975), pp. 262–72.

10. Maurice Bellet, 'Qui parle?' in *Christus* 83, Vol. 21 (June 1974), p. 305.

11. Yvonne Pellé-Douel, 'Paradoxes nécessaires', in *Christus* 72, Vol. 18 (October 1971), p. 519.

12. These two basic texts of St John of the Cross will be found in *The Ascent of Mount Carmel* II. 22, nos. 3–5 and *The Spiritual Canticle* II, nos. 3 and 6.

13. Hans-Jürgen Schultz, ed., *Wer ist das eigentlich—Gott?* (Munich, 1969), p. 20 (K Rahner), and p. 268 (J.-B. Metz).

14. If naming God is not to be a purely second-hand naming, it must come from prayer and spirituality. A very clear exposition of this idea is to be found in Joseph Ratzinger's *Dogma und Verkündigung* (Munich and Freiburg, 1973), pp. 117ff. He offers a very striking example which is relevant to our subject. The Latin word for redeemer or saviour is in fact *conservator*. For Christians, 'salvation' was, however, more than simply the preservation of Rome and of everything that existed from war, change or destruction. For them, salvation was related to the future and to history. The first Christians of Rome, then, did not use the word *conservator* for Christ, but *salvator* (*op. cit.*, pp. 94–95).

Piet Schoonenberg

# God as Person(al)

INTRODUCTION

ARE we bound to regard God as personal? This is in no sense a purely theoretical question. It is of course also theoretical and as such it calls for hermeneutics and above all a patient dialogue between East and West. But it is also a question that concerns every religious person and certainly every Christian in his deepest being. It concerns his prayer, his faith, his hope, the way in which the Christian message of 'God is love' is understood and the way in which he is able to love God with the whole of his heart.

In this article, an attempt is made to answer this question—an attempt that is, in my opinion, by no means closed. I begin by describing the possible meanings of the word 'person'. This description or definition will have to serve the dialogue between East and West and is provided as a contribution to that dialogue. It is important to bear in mind that we are not considering in the first place the word or concept of 'person' as such, but above all our understanding of God in two senses: firstly, how should we understand the word 'God' and, secondly, how are we to listen to the voice of God.

PERSON

Man is a person. Our whole being as men is in a state of becoming and we are therefore persons in a state of becoming. We are always struggling to become persons and to remain persons in the face of many threats of depersonalization. We have in mind an idea of being as persons and there has been a great deal of speculation about this idea in the West especially, so much, in fact, that even a historical account of this reflection would fill a book. In this article I can do no more than point to a few aspects of the concept 'person'. I will confine myself to three: identity, individuality and relationship.

*Identity.* He or she, that man or woman himself or herself, is a person. Even in cultures in which the concept 'person' has not been formed in reflective thought, a man is called by his name and calls himself by that name. By being addressed and called by his name he is someone and he is present. In classical antiquity, the words *prosōpon* and *persona* were used to indicate the part played by someone in a drama and to characterize him as the subject of speaking and action and therefore as someone with a right to a place among men: that is, as the subject of right. It is this view that underlies the patristic and scholastic definitions of 'person'. (See below.) Since the time of Kant, a great deal of thought has been given to the consciousness that the person has of himself and his freedom and responsibility, characteristics which are linked with that consciousness. Man is a person, then, in contrast to animals, plants and things, because his identity, his being himself, is realized in self-consciousness (being with himself) and freedom (being from himself). Man as a person says: I am I.

*Individuality.* By being an *I*, the person is not a generality, a species or another. This aspect of being a person is stressed in patristic and scholastic definitions. Boethius, for example, defined the person as *individua substantia rationalis naturae*. The person, then, was an individual substance. This sounds pleonastic to us today, of course, but the addition of 'individual' was an important one for Boethius, who wanted to delimit the person and distinguish him from the general beings (*ousiai*) of the Greek philosophers. The other addition of 'in a rational nature' enabled Boethius to apply the definition to man, the angels and God, although he did not perceive that this rational (or intellectual) nature raised being oneself to the level of consciousness of oneself.

Boethius' definition probably became classical because it emphasized a basic aspect of all being as a person, namely, individuality. In applying it to the Trinity, Richard of Saint Victor suggested an improvement: instead of *individua substantia*, he suggested *incommunicabilis existentia*, in other words, an existence that cannot be communicated (or rather, alienated), a being oneself that cannot be transferred to another. In this direction, Duns Scotus attributed an *ultima solitudo*, an ultimate loneliness, to the person. Being oneself always contains, then, the limitation of not being another and of never being able to become the other.

*Relationship.* The words 'incommunicable' and 'lonely' seem, however, to emphasize the negative aspect of being a person. There is a positive aspect which overcomes this—relationship. Every being is in a relationship with other beings. (I would go as far as to say that relationship to other beings *is* being.) This relationship, which characterizes being a person is not a relationship with a greater whole or with a generality, but one with a being 'over and against' the person, with objects and especially co-subjects and with other persons. This relationship makes someone a person if it is not simply a datum, but is engaged consciously and in freedom. Hegel above all was responsible for adding this idea of relationship to the Kantian concept of the person and since Hegel it has been regarded as a constitutive element. Hegel regarded the person as becoming concrete by entering into community with the other or by surrendering to the other. Man became a person by losing himself in the other. This view of the person has been stressed in philosophy and theology throughout this century, but especially between the wars, in the personalism of Ebner, Buber, Marcel and Nédoncelle. I am only I, I become I through my relationship, not with a him, a her or an it, but with a thou. I am I when I can say 'we'. Person exists in a community of persons.

We can sum up by saying that being a person is identity; it is consciously and freely itself, limited by individuality, but transcending this limitation in going out consciously and freely to the other. It should be clear from this definition that, as we said at the beginning of this article, man becomes a person.

## OUR QUESTION

Now that we have described and attempted to define 'person', we can ask this question: Can God be thought of as a person? In asking this question, we must take into account the Christian confession of faith in the Father, the Son and the Holy Spirit and the conviction that each of these is equally and identically God and that they have at the same time to be distinguished. In the West, this distinction has traditionally been expressed by the theological term 'three divine persons', to such an extent indeed, that only recently has God been called a person (in the singular). I would like to discuss here whether and to what degree the distinction between Father, Son and Holy Spirit can really be understood as a distinction between persons. At the same time, I will try to avoid speaking about the whole of the Trinity as a person. For this reason, the reader should understand the word 'God' in this article in the sense in which it is used in the New Testament, namely as God the Father. What is said about the Father as being or not being a person applies therefore to his relationship with us. I am not considering in this article interpersonal relationships between Father, Son and Holy Spirit, mainly because these do not destroy or even limit the Father's relationship with us.

More precisely formulated, then, our question is: Can God, the God of us Christians, 'the God and Father of our Lord Jesus Christ', be thought of as a person? The answer must be sought in the Christian experience of faith, as handed down to us in tradition and especially as expressed for the first time and fundamentally in Scripture. My reflections here will therefore be based mainly on the Old and New Testaments. I am, of course, aware of the plurality of theologies present in Scripture and will take this datum into account, but I believe too that there is a fundamental unity within that plurality.

Perhaps the most important problem, however, is this: what does the proclamation of God as a person in Scripture mean for us Christians today? Is it possible that a personal image of God in Scripture and later tradition is attributable to a past culture and way of thinking? If this is so, ought we, in our contemporary culture in which East and West are coming closer together, to find another image of God which is either less or not at all personal? Are we perhaps required to give up all our images of God and above all the personal image? We must try to answer this question as well. But first we must examine what Scripture has to tell us about this.

## GOD AS A PERSON IN SCRIPTURE

God is not called a person or personal anywhere in Scripture, since these words did not exist in the languages in which Scripture was written. If we read the Old Testament prophets, however, we recognize at once that they experienced God as personal. Yahweh had steadfast love for his people. He was jealous and angry in his love, but whenever his people turned back to him, he turned away from his anger. Those who attributed such human feelings to him were at the same time convinced that he was not a human being. They did not ascribe an unworthy anthropomorphism to God, but there is a clear contrast in this between the prophets and, for example, the Hellenistic thinkers. In the case of the latter, there was a tendency to strip the idea of God of all personal characteristics. Examples of this tendency are Aristotle's 'the prime mover' (in the neuter) and Plotinus' 'the one' (again in the neuter). The prophets, on the other hand, did not attribute other, less worthy human characteristics to God, such as vengefulness or lasting anger. 'I will not execute my fierce anger, I will not destroy . . ., for I am God and not man' (Hos 11:9)—but God is nonetheless described in this prophecy as a person.

To make this argument clearer, I propose to discuss the presence or absence of the three aspects of being a person outlined above (identity, individuality, relationship) in the biblical image of God. In this, I shall, of course, have to concentrate my attention mainly on the Yahwistic tradition, the prophets, the historical accounts inspired by the prophets and the gospels. The image of God in the Elohistic texts, the priestly tradition and the Wisdom literature (with the exception of the psalms) is less personal and certainly less 'involved'. I will try to indicate these nuances from time to time.

Let us begin with the aspect of *identity*. God is clearly identified by his name Yahwek, by which he was known to Israel 'since Egypt'. Exodus contains several stories in which God makes himself known as Israel's God by this name. I do not need to dwell on this point, as the author of the previous article deals with it at length. This name was, of course, replaced by Adonai (out of respect) and translated in the Septuagint as *ho kurios* ('the Lord'), but it was called out on the Day of Atonement by the high priest. There are also various personal titles, such as Lord, King and to some extent also Father, which was to have an entirely new content in the New Testament on the basis of Jesus' experience of God. The most personal term of address in the whole of Scripture is therefore 'Abba'. There is also evidence in the New Testament that Jesus' followers received the freedom (*parrhesia*) to address God with this title and that God pours the Spirit of his Son into our hearts so that we are able to cry: 'Abba, Father'.

In Scripture, then, we find that God is addressed as Yahweh, Lord and Father. What is more, he is represented as speaking himself and also acting, saving, choosing, having mercy and loving. This brings us to the aspect of *relationship*. This aspect is particularly stressed in Israel's experience of the covenant. It is very characteristic of Israel that covenants were concluded between men with regard to God and also that the whole relationship between the people and God was experienced as a covenant. Yahweh was Israel's God and Israel was Yahweh's people and, moreover, to such a degree that it became, not ethnically, but in the religious sense a unity (although this unity was, of course, relative). This covenant was recognized as the result of having been chosen by Yahweh and the Israelites also chose Yahweh several times as their God. The idea of the covenant was at times very strong, at others weak, but the formula 'I shall be their God and they will be my people' continued to be heard throughout the Bible as far as the Book of Revelation.

The covenant was attributed increasingly to Yahweh's initiative. This can be seen from the fact that the Hebrew *berîth* was translated as *diathēkē* in the Septuagint and as *testamentum* in the Vulgate. This shows clearly how the relationship was seen more and more as coming from Yahweh and going to the people and as emphasizing God's freedom as a person. God's attitudes in the Bible are above all such personal attitudes as grace, faithfulness and so on (see above). The replacement of the concept 'covenant' by 'kingdom' in the apocalyptic writings does not mean that the idea of God had become any less personal. On the contrary, this kingdom is also said, in the later apocalyptic works, to come about through God's initiative, without human intervention.

### GOD AS AN INDIVIDUAL?

In discussing the three aspects of being a person, I left out *individuality*, not primarily because this is limiting and to some extent negative, with the result that it can hardly be applied to God, but mainly because it is a difficult concept in Scripture as well. It is not constant and a certain development is noticeable in the Bible. Here above all we have to consider those parts of Scripture that I did not touch on above. In the first place, God is presented as an individual as Yahweh, that is, during the period when Israel was moving slowly from henotheism to monotheism before the exile. Yahweh was the only God for Israel, but it is clear that the gods of other peoples were recognized as such for them. This is apparent from a number of early texts, some of which were corrected later. Israel also recognized in its own prayers that Yahweh was the greatest of the gods. Even when Israel's faith was completely monotheistic and the alien gods had become nothing, *'ĕlohîm* continued to be used as a kind of specific name. The angels were called *beně-'ĕlohîm* and were regarded as specimens of the species *'ĕlohîm*. In this sense, then, Yahweh seems to have had an individual limitation.

All the same, attempts were clearly made in the Old Testament to break through this limitation without abandoning Yahweh's identity and his relationship with his people. His presence could not be limited by being confined to an image, but his name had to be invoked so that he might be present with his people. He revealed himself on Mount Sinai or Horeb and dwelt in the Temple on Mount Zion, but his real dwelling place came increasingly to be seen as heaven, the throne room above the vault of heaven. In his prayer of dedication of the Temple, Solomon clearly recognized that even heaven and the heaven of heavens could not contain God, but that his name dwelt in the Temple, so that he could listen to the entreaties of his people. The same applies to Yahweh's presence on earth. Both Naaman and David recognized that the land outside the territory belonging to the twelve tribes of Israel was the sphere of the other gods, but with the coming of monotheism the messianic hope arose that all peoples would come to Mount Zion and, from time to time, that Yahweh would be worshipped in Egypt and

Assyria and that a pure offering would be made to him from the East to the West (Isa 19:18–25; Mal 1:11).

Another attempt to remove all idea of limitation from the image of God was the attribution of actions to others than God himself. I have already pointed out briefly that the Elohist was less inclined to describe God as acting directly than the Yahwist. There are stories in the Old Testament in which God's guidance in a historical event is clearly proclaimed, but which give the impression that the event takes place by human factors. Examples of this are the Joseph story in Genesis and the books of Esther and Judith (in contrast to Jonah, for instance). Two ways of describing God's activity in order to stress his transcendence, however, are frequently found in the Old Testament—action that takes place through 'representatives' and the so-called *passivum divinum*.

In most ancient cultures, there are examples of men acting through someone who represents them and, in Hebrew thought, a representative of this kind was really an *alter ego*, an extension of the person who sends him to carry out the task.[1] The human person was present not only within his body, but also in his garments, his domestic possessions, his family and his descendants and above all in a servant sent by him (*šaliyaḥ, apostolos*). Yahweh frequently spoke, then, through his angel, who used the 'I' of Yahweh himself (Gen. 22:16) and in whom Yahweh's name dwelt (Exod. 23:21). In later Judaism just before and at the time of Jesus, when the apocalyptic type of writing was prevalent, God acted and spoke through many angels, although he continued to take the initiative. This is especially true of the Apocalypse of John. God is also personified in the Wisdom literature, in which divine wisdom is seen as his first creature and the executor of all his works as well as the radiation and image of his being. In rabbinism and the targums, God's action is ascribed to his Name, his Glory (*kabhôdh*), his dwelling (*šekhinah*), his word or his Spirit (*ruaḥ*). In the gospels and even in the words of Jesus himself, God is sometimes spoken of as wisdom, the heavens, power and so on.

Another way of indicating the mystery of God's action is by the use of the *passivum divinum*. The action is described in the passive and it is not said, but only suggested that the action is carried out by God. This way of speaking was used extensively by the apocalyptic authors and is found again and again in the books of Daniel and Revelation. A good example of this device is that of the breaking of the statue by a stone 'cut out by no human hand' in Nebuchadnezzar's dream (Dan. 2:34); this image is later interpreted as God's action to set up his kingdom (2:44). It is remarkable that this *passivum divinum* occurs at least a hundred times in the words of Jesus in the synoptic gospels and within them is attested by four traditions; it is for this reason that Jeremias has spoken of the *ipsissima vox Jesu* in these cases.[2]

In the context of the New Testament, we must consider the part played by the Holy Spirit, who is also a representative of God and the risen and glorified Christ. In the Old Testament, God sends his Spirit, but in the New Testament the Holy Spirit himself acts, especially in Acts and the Pauline letters. In and through this Spirit, however, God the Father was acting, especially in the Church and at the end of time. The Spirit is in this sense eschatologically God. The activity of the Spirit alternates not only with that of the Father, but also with that of the glorified Christ. A classical example of the latter is to be found in John 14, in which two comings, that of the Paraclete and that of Jesus, are juxtaposed and in which the Paraclete is, in Raymond Brown's words, 'another Jesus'[3] in his relationship with the disciples and the world. This is a clear case of 'representation'.

We have, then, found that God was regarded as personal by the biblical authors and especially in the prophetic books. He is 'Yahweh, your God'. He is characterized as a person by his identity and his relationship. Sometimes he seems to be individual in a human and therefore limited way—he is the God who is called Yahweh, the God 'of Israel'—and sometimes attempts are made to eliminate this limiting element from the idea of God. When this is done, he is presented as the universal God, the God of heaven who cannot be embraced, and as acting in man's history on earth without being absorbed by it and through the medium of representatives. His activity is, in other words, frequently suggested by the use of an impersonal passive.

All these modes of expression can be compared with those in which Yahweh or the Father of Jesus are presented in a very personal way. They do not, however, negate the personal presentation. On the contrary, God's personal relationship is again and again affirmed by this other mode of expression. The angel of Yahweh speaks to Abraham, after all, about the covenant. God's Name dwells among the people and his Wisdom spreads its roots among them.

If we examine Jesus' way of speaking in the New Testament, he seems on the one hand to name God frequently, calling him, for example, 'your heavenly Father', and, on the other, to have a preference for the *passivum divinum*. On the one hand, he speaks in a way that strikes us today as astonishingly direct about the heavenly Father feeding the birds, clothing the flowers, letting the sun shine and making the rain fall. On the other hand, he uses the *passivum divinum* to indicate God's comfort of the oppressed, his filling of the hungry, his opening of the door to those who knock and his giving of an overflowing measure.

In the Bible, then, God comes to us in his transcendence and his personal relationship. I should like to conclude this brief review by reflecting about two 'definitions' of God found in Johannine tradition: 'God is spirit' (John 4:24) and 'God is love' (1 John 4:8, 16). In the abstract, the first definition would fit easily into the idealism of the preceding century. But 'worshipping God in spirit and truth', the consequence of this definition, was in John's theology in no sense a purely interior form of adoration. It is not worship linked with Jerusalem or Mount Gerizim. It is rather the ultimate, universal form of worship envisaged in Isa. 19 and Malachi. 'God is spirit' therefore means in this context that God fills everything and breaks through all limitations. This does not, however, exclude God's personal relationship, since it is clear from the preceding verse that God is the Father who seeks such worshippers. According to John's theology, the Father is the one who gives Jesus everything that he does and loves both him and us. That Father is spirit and the reverse is also true: the Spirit is the Father.

God's being a spirit and his transcendence are even more closely united with his personal relationship in the second definition: 'God is love'. We always use imagery whenever we speak of God—not only when we call him a king or a warrior, following the Old Testament, but also when we follow Jesus' example and address him as father. Jesus' words about the Father who knows the Son and reveals everything to him are hidden parables about his relationship with God. The statement 'God is love' rises above this imagery, insofar as this is possible in human thought. It is at the same time the most personal statement that can be made about God. It is John's concise 'definition' of God for believers who know that he loved us and sent his Son to us. This statement can also serve in this article as the definition expressing both the unlimited nature of God and his being a person.

## OUR CONTEMPORARY WAY OF THINKING

How do we react, in the light of our contemporary way of thinking, to this scriptural image of God? In the first place, we are, I believe, on the way to liberating ourselves from the image of God as one of many gods, although he is the greatest, just as Israel liberated itself from the same image of Yahweh as one, although the greatest, of the gods. God who is unlimited cannot be one of many. He cannot be counted up or subsumed. Even during the scholastic period, God was not included within a species or genus. Hegel was confronted with the difficulty that, if God found limited beings in addition to himself, he could not himself be unlimited and infinite. This difficulty was reconsidered some years ago by Paul Tillich, who refused to speak of God as a being (another being) or as a person (another person). This type of thinking about God as a being in addition to other beings was given the name of 'theism' (it should be noted in passing that this use of the term implies a limitation in comparison with the original use of the same concept, according to which God was simply recognized). Tillich wanted to go beyond both this theism and atheism and, with this in mind, believed that even speaking about God as a person was misleading.[4]

I am inclined to share this conviction and to take his questions about our personal idea of God very seriously. I would therefore like to express this question in the form of a koan of the type used in Zen: 'What is the boundary if only one country is bounded?' The boundary 'between' us and God is only our boundary, not God's. The finite world and we who are in it cannot be outside God. He embraces everything and is everything, as Scripture seems to say at least once (*hū' hakkôl, tō pan estin autos*, 'He is all'; Ecclus. 43:27). On the other hand, this does not mean that finite being is absorbed or destroyed—on the contrary, it remains distinct from God and limited with regard to him. We are therefore confronted by the mystery that both the scholastic doctrine of participation and modern forms of pan-en-theism have attempted to express. It is hardly surprising that we are impressed by this mystery nowadays, partly under the influence of eastern thought. This has made us more critical of the idea of speaking about and to God as a person. The author of Ps. 139 did not know where to turn to find God, since he was everywhere. We share his difficulty in a heightened form. Why, we ask, do we still pray to God, believe in him and hope in him, if he is so identified with us in his unlimited nature that we can no longer think of him as over and against us?

There are two possible answers to this question. We can set aside the whole scriptural way of thinking and the long tradition of teaching about God as a person. This means casting overboard the whole Jewish-Christian tradition or calling the personal image of God that it contains historically conditioned. The second solution is to try to find a synthesis and this is the solution that I shall seek in the pages that follow, since we cannot as Christians abandon the personal image of God and we do not need to do this, because both Scripture and the tradition of the Church point the way to a synthesis.

We cannot as Christians abandon the personal image of God. The first reason why we cannot do this is because we would in that case no longer be able to see God as freedom. If he is not freedom, then there is no reason for believing that the distinction between God and the world is real. In that case, the existence of the world is illusory and we have to liberate ourselves from this, or else it is simply an empty word. The second reason intimately affects our experience of faith and may therefore be the only valid reason for us as Christians. It also touches the whole question of God's revelation in Christ Jesus. It is not so important that our abandonment of a personal image of God would entail an abandonment of Jesus' favourite term of address: 'Abba, Father', since that was in the last resort, also an image. What it would involve, if we were no longer to see God as a person, is an abandonment of the whole interrelationship between God and Jesus and of the implications of the Johannine definition: 'God is love'. God would no longer be greater than our hearts and his love would no longer enable us to hope against hope. He would no longer be the love that he was for Jesus on the cross. I believe that, if we were unable to call God love, we would have to conclude with Paul that our faith was in vain and we would still be in our sins.

We do not need to abandon the personal image of God, because, in the light of Scripture, we are already on the way towards stripping this personal image of God of the anthropomorphism of limiting individuality. We can include the scriptural image of God in our western way of thinking and in the dialogue between East and West that is increasing nowadays. In this way it would be purified. As we pointed out above, the boundary 'between' God and ourselves is not God's boundary. The interpersonal relationship between God and us and the corresponding relationship between ourselves and him cannot therefore be experienced in accordance with the image of two human persons who, in their limitations, are over and against one another and who reach out to each other from their mutual limitation and 'ultimate loneliness'. He is 'all' and already with us. His immanence precedes his condescension. But he is also transcendent and 'over and against' us as freedom and love, as the promise of a greater community and he is, in and from Jesus, on the way towards becoming 'all in all'.

I hope that it will be clear by now that the *word* 'person' is not the most important aspect of my argument, which is mainly concerned with the identity and relationship and even more with the freedom and love of God. We are, however, bound to deny the limiting individuality that we spontaneously connected with the first two aspects with regard to God. Indeed, the word 'person' can even be omitted from our speaking about God, although I would not myself do this. (That is why I have left the title of this article open and provided a choice between the noun 'person' and the adjective 'personal'.) In any case, it is clear that our concept 'person' has to be purified if we are to apply it to God. It will also have to be purified if we use it when we direct ourselves *to* him. Prayer is speaking to God, certainly, but it is not speaking to someone who is *simply* the other and over and against us. Praying is raising one's heart to God, certainly, but also knowing that he is present in the depths of our heart. When we pray, we make ourselves open to the God who is already penetrating us everywhere and who wants to fill us more and more. Praying is opening ourselves to the Other, who, in his freedom, is never our possession, but who bears us in his love. Prayer is directing ourselves towards the one who is over and against us and who is already present in our subjectivity, because his Spirit prays in us with sighs too deep for words.

### DIALOGUE WITH THE EAST

In this article I have mentioned the dialogue between East and West several times. In my opinion, a great deal of time, patience and study will have to be devoted to this, if we are to understand and enrich each other in the matter of the content of the concept 'person' and our way of thinking about God as person(al). But in the meantime, this dialogue has to begin—indeed, it has already begun. This number of *Concilium* is a contribution to it and I hope that this article is also a contribution to it. I shall therefore conclude this article with a few remarks that refer directly to this dialogue. As I am not a specialist in Asiatic languages or religions, I shall confine myself to the available books and articles on the subject and above all to an article by P. Nemeshegyi, in which he summarizes the ideas of several theologians working in Japan and India.[5]

These scholars have clearly reflected on both God's and man's being as a person. Above, I have tried to liberate God's being as a person from the limitations of individuality. These Japanese and Indian thinkers, however, begin with man. Obviously inspired by Eastern mysticism, they make a distinction between the *I* and the 'self'. A third step is added to Buber's well-known distinction: '*I*-it', '*I*-thou' and '*I*-in-thee-in-me'. The first stage is that of the possessive, egoistic *I*. The *I* of the second stage is not egoistic and that of the third is called 'non-egotic'. What is particularly striking, then, is how man arrives, in the thought of these Asiatic Christians, at a non-egotic being as a person not simply by sinking down, but above all by love (*agape*). They think of this non-egotic being as a person as a being as a person of which only God is worthy. It has, however, been achieved at the human level in Jesus Christ and can be achieved in us in that we conform to him.

This seems to me to be a surprising and rich contribution to the dialogue about God's being as a person and ours. It is also possible that it is taking a biblical idea a stage further. According to the fourth gospel, Jesus said: 'Who sees me, sees the Father'. Can this not be applied to Jesus, who washed the disciples' feet and gave himself to us, going as far as death? In the dying Jesus, we see the Father's *I*, not egoistic and non-egotic, but as purely giving and self-communicating love. The '*I*-am' of Exodus is realized in the death of Jesus on the cross: 'When you have lifted up the Son of Man, then you will know that I am he' (John 8:27).

Let us return to the East. It is possible that this attribution of a 'non-egotic being as a person' may give a deeper content to the *advaita* or non-duality between God and the world. It is emphasized nowadays that the idea of *advaita* is not a form of monism, but that it is simply a refusal to call God and the world either one or two. Is this a historical interpretation of the great philosopher of Hinduism, Śankara, or is the relationship between this idea and Śankara similar to that between transcendental Thomism and Thomas Aquinas?

This is not really very important, since this insight into the non-duality which is a non-unity is in any case very enriching. We owe a great debt to Raimundo Pannikar for his propagation of this interpretation of the *advaita* doctrine in various publications.[6] I am bound, however, to ask whether Pannikar is really consistent in placing the *jnana* or 'knowledge' of this *advaita* above the personal relationship or *devotio* to God (*bhakti*).[7] I am also bound to ask whether—if neither unity nor duality is the last word for the relationship between God and the world or God and man—we should not seek a higher unity between unity and duality, a synthesis of identity and alterity and therefore of *jnana* and *bhakti*. Are the mysticism of unity and that of interpersonal relationships always mutually complementary? Can the *advaita* experience of Hinduism be recognized in the 'O-Thou-I' of Al-Hallaj? These are questions that I am not qualified to answer, but they are important for the dialogue between East and West and indeed for the whole of our reaching out towards God in thought.

*Translated by David Smith*

## Notes

1. See Aubrey R. Johnson, *The One and the Many in the Israelite Conception of God* (Cardiff, 1961).

2. Joachim Jeremias, *Neutestamentliche Theologie*, I (Gütersloh, 1973), pp. 20–74.

3. Raymond E. Brown, *The Gospel according to John*, II (Anchor Bible, 29A) (Garden City, 1966), pp. 1135–44.

4. Paul Tillich, *Systematic Theology*, I, chapter x (c).

5. Petrus Nemeshegyi, 'Versuch über Einkulturierung des Christentums in

Asien', in *Internationale Theologenkommission. Die Einheit des Glaubens und der theologische Pluralismus* (Einsiedeln, 1973), pp. 180–203. On pp. 186–88, the author summarizes works by K. Takizawa (Japan) and Sunder Rao and Surjat Singh (India).

6. See, for example, his *The Trinity and the Religious Experience of Man: Icon-Person-Mystery* (New York and London, 1973), p. 36.

7. *Ibid.*, p. 31ff.

Frans Maas

# A Personal or Impersonal God—An Old Problem of Western Mysticism?

ALL western mystics display an ever stronger longing for God. They are content with nothing less than God himself. No traces of God in his creation, no visions, no good life well lived, nothing other than God himself can assuage their longing. The question we are concerned with here is whether this 'God himself' of mystical experience can throw any light on the theme of this issue of *Concilium*: namely, the 'personal God'.

The editors suggested that I should make a distinction between two tendencies in western mysticism: 'natural' mysticism and 'bridal' or 'nuptial' mysticism.

*Natural mysticism:* in the history of men's experience of transcendent striving towards God there is an apparent return to the source; a return to what man has been from all eternity and has never ceased to be: God is the inexpressible meaning of the original unity of all things; unity between God and man has to be sought after, as if in an odyssey.

*Bridal mysticism:* a spiritual evolution is described in terms of a personal model: the relationship between God and man is expressed as that between the Bridegroom and his bride, as in the Song of Solomon; God is the inexpressible meaning of ultimate union; created unity, as in Exodus.

It seems as if the emphasis on God himself in natural mysticism is more inclined to an impersonal, and in bridal mysticism to a personal model. We have to ask if this stress is appropriate, and whether the distinction between natural and bridal mysticism is as relevant to our topic as might at first seem to be the case.

I shall examine the question in terms of two representative figures: Meister Eckhart (?1260–1327) for natural mysticism, and St John of the Cross (1542–1591) for bridal mysticism. The conventional approach would be to offer a definition of the concept 'person' and then to see how far the God-notions of the two mystics accorded with it. In order to avoid the danger of an arbitrary definition, I shall not follow that course. Instead I shall look in some detail at what Eckhart has to say about God himself, before going on to John of the Cross; at appropriate points I shall examine the relevance of what Eckhart says to our present topic.

MEISTER ECKHART

In Eckhart the person image gradually gives way to a largely spatial form of imagery: God himself is the location of original unity. Is there such a thing as a non-personal notion of God in Eckhart? Not so baldly, for not even the highest stage of mystical experience decides the form of the God-concept. Or, to put it another way, an understanding of God emerges in the course of the mystical journey and is carried forward into the final stage. I shall now try to decide to what extent that ultimate suprapersonal notion of God in Eckhart's works is in fact personal.

## Separation from God

'The highest and ultimate thing that a man can abandon is to abandon God for God's sake'. '. . . what I am not, that God also should not be; I am then the cause of God being "God"'. 'God becomes "God"; where all creatures express God, God comes into being'. 'We declare that wherever God is no more than "God", he is not the highest end of creation'.

At first these propositions seem quite extraordinary, but they have to be understood in the setting of the purification which Eckhart is trying to convey in the manner of speculative philosophy. Purification in his German writings is often 'separation' or 'detachment', a mode of dissent. It is to be thought of primarily as detachment on a moral and ascetic level. A man has to separate himself from everything that is not God himself. 'Know that whenever in one way or another you search for your own end, you will never find God if God is all that you are searching for'. All kinds of religiously qualified actions, such as keeping watch, fasting, following a holy rule of life, doing good works, and so on, can be done for one's own sake. Self-interest can take unsuspected forms which bring one to a stop rather than promote spiritual progress.

Eckhart's constant summons to abandon everything that is not God himself is issued against the background of a conviction that 'all creatures are pure nothing. I do not mean that they are of little value or that they are something of some kind. They are pure nothing'. This conviction is rooted in an originally neo-Platonic intuition: oneness. God is the One and without the One he is nothing. The creation is fragmentation from the One, a splintering in time and space, and as such nothing. Through creation a gulf is brought about between God the creator and his creature. God becomes 'God', inasmuch as created things look up to him and address him as 'God'. God is seen to exist as the God without: 'God is in all things. The more he is in things, the more he is outside things; the more he is within, the more he is without'.

Purification or refinement means departure from all creatureliness, even from one's own created being. Eckhart takes this separation to the radical point of separation from the Creator. Separation in this sense, however, is compared with a son's leavetaking of his father which he needs must undergo if he is to reach maturity. Another analogy is a servant's departure from his master when he wishes to become independent. Mature service to God demands separation from God as creator.

## God's birth in the soul

In order to discover what real existence means for Eckhart, we must examine one of his central themes: God's birth in the soul: 'It is necessarily true that similarity and fervent love draw up and lead and bring the soul into the first source of the One, who is the Father of all in heaven and on earth. So I say then that similarity, begotten of the One, draws the soul into God, as he is one in his hidden unity, for that is the meaning of "one" . . . according as the soul is more pure, denuded and poor, and the less she has of the creatures and the more she is empty of all things which are not God, the more purely she receives God, the more she is in God and the more she becomes one with God'.

Separation from God outside and above mankind is not absolute separation, but rather a 'leavetaking of God for the sake of God'. This kind of departure opens up the perspective of inwardness. We see no longer as it were above or without, but now within, where our soul is truly like unto God as to nothing in the world: 'God and I are one'. Eckhart cites Augustine in pointing out that God is more intimate with me than I am with myself. Separation from God opens up the way to the soul.

## The necessity of God's birth

When man takes his leave of creation and thus approaches inward being and outward nothingness, 'To be empty of all creatures is to be full of God, and to be full of all creatures is to be empty of God. You should know also that in this immovable detachment God has dwelt eternally and he still dwells in it. And you should know that when God created heaven and earth and all creatures, that affected his immovable detachment as little as if the creatures had never been created . . . Everything that God works in all the saints, God works in the innermost of the soul. The Father begets his Son in the innermost of the soul, and begets you with his only-begotten Son as not less than Him. If I am to be a son, I must be a son in the same being in which He is the Son and in no other. If I am to be a man, I cannot be a man in the being of an animal, but I must be a man in the being of a man. But if I am to be this man, i.e. the man who is called to be a son of God by grace and adoption, I must be this man in this being. For St John says, "You are sons of God"'. 'God became man through and through in order that he might beget you as his only-begotten Son and not less'. 'God's nature, his being and his Godhead depend on his action in the soul'.[1]

Eckhart locates the centre of reality in the soul. He speaks not so much of free communication between God and man as of a necessary birth of God's Son in the soul of man. 'God is so bound and held that he can do only what that man wishes', says Eckhart of the God-attuned man. He does not of course conceive of any kind of personal human power over God but of the necessity which comes from oneness between God and man: '"Thy will be done". But it would be better to say: "Be the will thine; may my will become His will, may I become He"'; that is what the Our Father means.

The heart of reality is not dependent on freedom. The freedom which is generally taken as an essential component of being-a-person is for Eckhart not to be predicated of a religious relationship between God and man; it is characteristic neither of one nor of the other. If the idea of personality is essentially bound up with the notion of freedom of the will, then the *fundamental* characteristic of Eckhart's experience of God would be the non-personal nature of God. Eckhart allows the understanding a higher place than the will as a means of access to this fundamental aspect of the experience of God.

## The dynamic nature of the birth of God

Nevertheless Eckhart does offer a Trinitarian and personal description of the birth of God. The Trinitarian process affects the soul: 'The

Father utters the Word and speaks in the Word and not otherwise than in that Word; but Jesus speaks in the soul. He speaks so that he reveals himself and everything that the Father uttered in him'.

The Father expresses himself in the Word and keeps nothing of himself back from the Word. The Word is the Son, the second Person, and through the Son the soul also becomes the Word. God is originally all in all through the Son. As the Son, God is an inward-immanent God (*intus totus*). As the Father, he is more a transcendent God (*extra totus*). The dynamic nature of the birth of God in the soul consists in the fact that God-in-me is always approaching the condition of God-outside-me. This dynamic process is the third Person, the Spirit: 'The Holy Spirit's attribute is that he did not come from the Father by procreation, but sprang from Father and Son alike, not by way of creation, but by love'. 'When the soul is gathered up in God's loving embrace it rises up and stands in perfect bliss and beauty. The senses are mute. The knowledge of God becomes immediate and independent of visual impressions. When the soul has reached this pure realization of God, it knows him in his unity of nature and trinity of Persons. His will and the soul's will are caught up in the same current, embracing in real union, touching and becoming as one: God has given the soul some of his divine essence. He considers the creature and infuses it with his nature, whilst the soul contemplates God and receives from him its true character. God is present where I am, and wherever he is, I am to be found. What is his is also mine and as I love all that is mine and my love is returned, I am being drawn into the loved Object and absorbed by it. Through love we become divine in union with God as far as creatures can achieve this. What God is by nature, the soul is by grace'.

Created things mean fragmentation in time and space, whereas detachment from them is the beginning of the way back to God. And that beginning of the way lies in the human soul. Eckhart conceives that return in the form of man being taken up into the Trinitarian process in which the Son is received in the Spirit into the Father. The return appears as a dynamic unity. The need for personal imagery, however, causes that process to be depicted as an interpersonal process: God is shown as a person in the intimate imagery of giving birth and being born.

## God and Godhead

But 'God is hidden in the ground of the soul where God's ground and the ground of the soul are one'. The dynamics of oneness extends beyond the birth of God, to what Eckhart calls 'nobility of soul' and 'breaking through into Godhead'.

## Nobility of soul

'The sixth stage is when man is transformed and conformed by God's eternity and has reached full and complete forgetfulness of this transient and temporal life and is drawn and transformed into the divine image and has become a child of God. There is no stage beyond this or higher, and here there is eternal rest and bliss, for the end of the inward man and of the new man is eternal life'. The highest nobility of soul otherwise is when God is present in his suprapersonal uniqueness. Eckhart's term for that is 'Godhead': 'God is in the ground of the soul with all his Godhead'. The theme of the distinction between 'God' and 'Godhead' is bound up with that of 'breakthrough'.

## Breaking through to Godhead

Whenever Eckhart makes a distinction between God and Godhead he of course does not claim any real distinction within God himself. In God, God and Godhead are one. God is creator and the outward aspect; Godhead is the aspect of unity. Godhead is God in his absoluteness, in his uniqueness. Godhead is the ground of God's unfolding in three persons. As Godhead God is one but not active; as God God is outwardly active, unfolding himself in Trinity and creatively. Hence his outgoingness from his oneness. In nobility of soul man breaks through to that originality of Godhead, not by man's own power but through God's loving kindness, through necessary grace.[2]

'The more man strives to be receptive of the divine inflowing, the happier he is, and whoever can place himself in the highest preparedness for it also dwells in the highest happiness. Now no man can make himself receptive of the divine inflowing except by uniformity with God . . . If anyone wishes to attain perfect detachment, let him strive for perfect humility, then he will come close to the Godhead'. In the very innermost essence of the soul man breaks through into eternity and is caught up into Deity, becoming what he originally was in God before creation. Personal union becomes mystical union: a suprapersonal unity which existed before the Creation. In the beginning God and man were 'not alike but one'.

Ultimately, in Eckhart's absolute terminology, God seems more like a place, a location, than a person. To attain to this one, unique, illimitable God-himself 'behind God's back' is the mystic's desire and aim. God's ground and the soul's ground are one. The profound heart of reality is unspeakable, though Eckhart refers to it as still, obscure and spacious. Hence: 'The best that a man can say about God is that he can be silent by reason of his innermost riches':

We come back to the initial question: Is Eckhart's notion of God personal or impersonal? Experience is essentially coloured by terminology, and Eckhart's is neo-Platonic in the sense that everything is in regard to the One. If God's being-a-person necessarily implies his being over-against the human person, then he is not a person. Nothing is over against God. Inasmuch as being-a-person implies volitional freedom, God is not a person. The original-unique unity of God and man was characterized by negation of the Trinitarian-personal movement: 'I must know God as he is: non-God, non-spirit, non-person, non-image . . . one and free of all division'.

The denial of God's being-a-person is not the same as asserting that he is not a person. God is above all images; not only above all personal imagery but above all non-personal atheistic God-imagery. The denial in question is only meaningful if it goes that far. The notion of person that Eckhart refutes is that of a divided person, but in the sense that what is refuted is assumed, or sublated, into the new conception. Hence the suprapersonal God gathers up all the personal intensity and richness of the process of conception in which such a term as person has lost its meaning. But the new significance depends on that loss of meaning. The heart of reality is indeed suprapersonal, but it may indeed be approached in a personal perspective.

## ST JOHN OF THE CROSS

The imagery which St John of the Cross uses to describe his mystical experience is essentially personal. It is the figure of two lovers who after many vicissitudes develop a profound union of love. In the *Spiritual Canticle* the image is to the fore, but it is also present in the other works. The personal nature of St John's concept of God is clear from the way in which he describes man's free transition through grace to union: 'In this matter, however, it is well to note clearly the difference that exists between the possession of God through grace itself alone and the possession of him through union; for the one consists in deep mutual love, but in the other there is also communication. There is as great a difference between these states as there is between betrothal and marriage. For in betrothal there is only a consent by agreement, and a unity of will between the two parties, and the jewels and the adornment of the bride-to-be, given her graciously by the bridegroom. But in marriage there is likewise communication between the persons, and union' (*Living Flame of Love*, III, 24).

The personal model does not of course prevent St John from saying on a number of occasions that God lies outside any image or form: '. . . God comes not within any image or form, neither is contained within any particular kind of intelligence' (*Ascent of Mount Carmel*, II, 16, 7). There are many remarks in his works about the inconceivability of God, and God's inexpressible nature. Yet the experience of God for him is best understood as a developing encounter between two persons. From the self-evident proposition that God is a person, he derives a narrative of the relation between God and man which is described primarily though not always in interpersonal terms.

## God apparent through the world

The *Spiritual Canticle* contains a relevant text in which the Beloved (God) dwells in the bride (the soul). The soul encounters the creation (which, for St John the lyric poet, is nature) in the process of pursuit. Created things are God's traces, and in that sense are signs more of his absence than of his presence; hence they cause the soul pain, for they are not God himself. The soul must continue its pursuit. The place of encounter comes into sight: a mountain, a garden, and so on. When the soul reaches the Beloved, the soul also finds everything it sought on her way to him: '. . . in that which God is wont to communicate in such excesses the soul feels and knows the truth of that saying which Saint Francis uttered, namely: "God mine, and all things". Wherefore, since God is all things to the soul, and the good of them all, the communication of this excess is explained by the similitude of the goodness of the things in the said stanzas, which we shall expound line by line. Herein must be understood that all that is expounded here is in God in an eminent and infinite manner, or, to express it better, each of these grandeurs which are spoken of is God, and then are all of them God; for, inasmuch as in this case the soul is united with God, it feels that all things are God, even as Saint John felt when he said: *Quod factum est, in ipso vita erat.* That is to say: That which was made in him was life. It is not to be understood that, in that which the soul is here said to feel, it is, as it were, seeing things in the light, or creatures in God, but that in that possession the soul feels that all things are God to it. Neither is it to be understood that, because the soul has such lofty feelings concerning God in that which we are saying, it sees God essentially and clearly, for this is no more than a powerful and abundant communication, and a glimpse of that which he is in himself, wherein the soul feels this goodness concerning the things which we shall expound in these lines, as follows: "My Beloved, the mountains". The mountains have height; they are abundant, extensive and beautiful, graceful, flowery and fragrant. These mountains my Beloved is to me.' (*Spiritual Canticle*, 14–15, 5–7).[3] And: '. . . it is true that the soul is now able to see that these things are distinct from God, inasmuch as they have a created being, and it sees them in him, with their force, root and strength; it knows equally that God, in his own Being, is all these things, in an infinite and pre-eminent way, to such a point that it understands them better in his Being than in themselves' (*Living Flame of Love*, 4, 5).

It is important to note that in the experience of the soul united with God, God remains a person, but also takes on the appearance of the world. When man gets close to the heart of reality, and looks out from that vantage point, he sees everything in its real truth: as nothing other than God. In that experience God is still a person, but this personal quality extends to everything round the mystic. The everyday reality that formerly was marked by the absence of God now becomes personal: 'For me my Beloved is the mountain'.

St John of the Cross extends the personal sphere, just as Eckhart refutes the 'purely personal'. The personal note enables man to see God in all things. The transition to the interpersonal mode does not lead to an impersonal cosmic indwelling of Deity, but to a personal-divine quickening of the cosmos. The soul sees: 'God, whose face is full of graces of all the creatures and of terrible power and glory and whose voice is the multitude of his excellences' (*Living Flame of Love*, 4, 11).

## God as the eccentric centre of the soul

Another group of texts calls God the soul's centre. In the commentary on the verse, 'Oh, living flame of love, that tenderly woundest my soul in its deepest centre', St John uses the image of the stone. For '. . . a stone, when in some way it is within the earth, is in some way in its centre, and this although it be not in the deepest part of the earth, because it is within the sphere of its centre and activity and movement; but we shall not say that it is in its deepest centre, which is the middle of the earth, and therefore it still has power and force and inclination to descend and to attain to this farthest and deepest centre if that which impedes it be taken away; and when it attains to its centre and there remains to it no more power and inclination of its own to move farther, we shall say that it is in its deepest centre' (*Living Flame of Love*, 1, 11). It cannot move from this deepest point, the centre of the earth: 'The centre of the soul is God; and, when the soul has attained to him according to the whole capacity of its being, and according to the force of its operation and inclination, it will have reached its last and deepest centre in God, which will be when with all its powers it understands and loves and enjoys God and, so long as it has not attained as far as this, as is the case in this mortal life, wherein the soul cannot attain to God with all its power, then, although it be in this its centre, which is

God, by grace and by his own communication which he has with it, still, inasmuch as it has the power of movement and strength to go farther, and is not satisfied, then, although it may be in the centre, it is nevertheless not in the deepest centre, since it is capable of going to the deepest centre of God' (*Living Flame of Love*, 1, 12).

In this way, St John portrays the soul and its longing. It is looking for God. God remains a person. God is the space within which man can reach his deepest self. God is the innermost profundity of the soul. In that sense God is no longer another person. Or, rather: God is also another, and outside man when a man's innermost self lies outside God.

### SUMMARY: NATURAL AND BRIDAL MYSTICISM

In bridal mysticism God is more personal and there is a greater emphasis on God's personal action through grace than we find in natural mysticism. Yet both types of mysticism stress the personal nature of God, each in its own way. Eckhart emphasizes the inward aspect, whereas St John of the Cross is stronger on the outward aspect.[4] The distinction between natural and bridal mysticism is relevant to the mystical journey to God himself. The symbolic structure is different in each case, as is the direction of the journey. But as the pilgrimage nears its goal, the distinction loses its relevance. For both forms of mysticism, God himself is there where God is at home, and where everyone and everything are assumed, in the one case in terms of the notion of original unity, in the other in the figure of ultimate union. Accordingly, we may say that for both mystics and mystical traditions, God himself is beyond the dilemma of the 'personal or impersonal' Deity.

*Translated by J. Maxwell*

### Notes

1. Cf. Shizuteru Ueda, 'Über den Sprachgebrauch Meister Eckharts "Gott muss . . ."', in Gerhard Müller and Winfried Zeller (eds.), *Glaube, Geist, Geschichte. Festschrift für Ernst Benz* (Leiden, 1967), pp. 266–79. In the general area of the present theme, Ueda offers an outstanding analysis of Eckhart's notion of God, and mediates Eastern and Western ideas. Nevertheless, I should say that for Eckhart the personal-triune God occupies a more central position in Eckhart than Ueda would allow. See also, A. Brounts, 'Hadewijchs eerste ontwerp van de wezensmystiek' in *Handelingen* 26 (1972), p. 52.

2. See Vladimir Lossky, 'Théologie négative et connaissance de Dieu chez Maître Eckhart', in *Etudes de Philosophie Médiévale* 48 (Paris, 1960), pp. 342–44.

3. It is interesting to note how many translators of St John of the Cross are intent to avoid translating any identification of God and world out of fear of pantheism. See J. Bendiek, 'Gott und Welt nach Johannes vom Kreuz', in *Philosophisches Jahrbuch* 79 (1972), pp. 88–105.

4. 'Introverted and extroverted mysticism' according to W. T. Stace, *Mysticism and Philosophy* (Philadelphia and New York, 1960), pp. 131–3.

# PART IV

*The Religious and Political Relevance
of God as a Personal Being*

Georg Wildmann

# The Personal Notion of God
# as a Condition of the History
# of Freedom in the West

'WORLD history is progress in awareness of freedom'. In this state-ment Hegel recapitulated his philosophy of history and defined the es-sence of history as freedom realized in events. In the present outline I take up Hegel's suggestion in order to inquire into one of the essential conditions of the history of freedom: the understanding of God as per-son. What is involved is an historical investigation of the question whether a personal understanding of God was an essential condition for the growth, in an historical process, of Western man's awareness of himself as a free subject able to live this freedom as a mandate to con-trol nature and as a right to individual development within society. This treatment of the question is restricted to an inquiry into the potency of the Judaeo-Christian heritage for the creation of freedom.

### GUIDING HYPOTHESES

The theme falls within the sphere of empirical reason and responds therefore to the historico-hermeneutical method. Historical hermeneu-tics, however, also needs hypotheses to test its conclusions.[1] The first hy-pothesis belongs to comparative religion and states that there is a corre-lation between the understanding of God and the understanding of man: man tries to understand himself in the light of God. The second hypothesis is derived from Max Weber's sociology of religion and as-serts that the understanding of God and the understanding of man are 'embodied' in social structures; that the image of God and of man is displayed in political dimensions; it has potency and relevance in regard to structural formation. The third hypothesis asserts that the institutional reality falls short of the 'idea' which it is supposed to embody. For a variety of reasons, which cannot be examined here, the 'idea' derived from the understanding of God and of man cannot be adequately converted into social reality. Hence, by analogy with the theory of 'cultural lag',[2] we can speak of an 'institutional' or 'structural lag'.

### THE LIBERATING GOD OF THE OLD TESTAMENT

Within the framework of comparative religion, we can find an internal coherence in the Old Testament if the idea of the liberating God is the central point of reference. According to the correlation hypothesis, God understood as personal and free brings about the awakening of the consciousness of freedom in Old Testament man. God is understood as a Thou, freely calling and choosing men to enter into a covenant. Man feels that he is regarded by God as a free partner, for it is only thus that he can make a covenant. He is described as the image of God immediately after God has revealed himself as creator and chooser. As a projection of God's creative freedom he is to rule the earth. In the ninth chapter of Genesis man's resemblance to God is given as the reason for his inviolability. In this way, two decisive factors are introduced into the history of freedom: man's right to control the world and the uncontrollability of human existence. The 'structural lag' is shown in the fact that the people did not succeed in setting up a direct rule of God. What was produced was a kingdom which soon acquired the features of surrounding despotisms. The quest for a full unity of God's dominion in man's dominion meant that the hope of the devout was expressed in the idea of a Messiah.

### JESUS' FREEDOM-CREATING ACTIVITY

These historical circumstances make it clear that, if anyone appeared with a messianic claim, he would have to take up the idea of the liberating God but at the same time would have to accept the historical inevitability of two effective liberating factors. First, he would have to submit the pure legalism of the contemporary relationship to God to criticism and oppose it with a morality of love. Jesus then in his human existence—and this corresponds to the correlation hypothesis—lived the liberating God and portrayed the presupposition of any social freedom: existentially free subjectivity. Second, he would have to fight against the nationalistically constricted idea of God's rule. The thrust of Jesus' action and talk was therefore directed also at God's total claim on all nations and on the cosmos as a whole. This is confirmed in the first reflection of the Christ-event in Paul and John, which is then expanded into a liberating deed of cosmic dimensions. The Kingdom of God is seen as the liberation of the whole cosmos.

### THE INCARNATION AND THE TRINITY IN CHRISTIAN ANTIQUITY

The death of Jesus was also a criminal's death imposed by the legitimate authority of the State. By raising this political outcast from the dead, God repudiated the authority of the State and the Roman religion which sustained it. God desacralized the Emperor and charged his Son to overcome the evil aeon. Christians drew the conclusion that Christ Jesus was the true Kyrios. They became aware that the community of Christ's followers had a right to regard itself as a social entity independent of the State and free to follow its Lord. This abolition of the coincidence of politics and religion reveals the basis for religious freedom. In addition, the community can identify itself with the socially disadvantaged, those described in the Bible as the 'poor'. In principle, therefore, social criticism of State and society is possible. The community can go further and obey God rather than man, thus becoming aware in principle of freedom of conscience.

The 'Constantinian turning-point', which is so often deplored, represents a 'structural lag' inasmuch as Constantine the Great forced the Church to become an imperial Church. Christianity had to take over the function of the ancient religion; to be the foundation of the State and co-protector of its culture.

With the Chalcedonian definition, the Christian image of God acquired an additional socio-critical force. If it can be assumed that there are three persons in the Godhead, living in free, equal and loving fellowship, then man can enter into a creative dialogue with any one of them. Moreover, according to the correlation hypothesis, it cannot be long before the new concept of person is applied to man. The implications for freedom were inherent in Boethius' definition of person as the individual existence in itself of a rational nature. A person can never be merely the function of another individual, or of the community. A person exists for the sake of his own perfection.

### THE IMAGE OF THE PERSONAL GOD IN MEDIEVAL EUROPE

At first it seems strange that Christendom was not built on a structural basis of free and loving subjectivity. The feudal system of the Middle Ages bears clear signs of a 'cultural lag'. The new image of God and man was interpreted with the inadequate aid of Roman and Germanic ideas of rule and law. Man enjoyed only functional liberties, the *libertates* which belonged to him in virtue of his status by birth. But each of the historically effective groups at this time attributed the initiative in salvation, according to its own preference, to one of three persons in God and thus regarded itself existentially as committed more to the Father, more to the Son or more to the Holy Spirit. This brought them into imperial and ecclesiastical political conflicts from which resulted a dynamism of freedom which prepared the way for modern times. That is to say: without the dynamism of ideas arising from the triune personality of God, the history of the Middle Ages would be unintelligible. Consequently there was theological authorization for the attempt on the part of the conflicting formative forces of this epoch—already programmatically formulated in Christian antiquity in the Letter to Diognetus—to be soul and leaven of the whole empire.

Anselm of Canterbury's theory of redemption places the Father at the centre of the economy of salvation. The theory is worked out in the light of the liberties attributed by scholastic trinitarian theology to the divine persons. There is an analogous contractual economy in the liberties of the different estates. The upholders of the feudal system consequently prefer an existential commitment to God the Father.

With Gregory VII's 'papal revolution' the freedom-creating function of the cross of Christ again came to the fore and necessitated the end of 'Constantinianism'. The popes themselves—instead of the emperors—from now on were called *vicarii Christi* and regarded themselves as trustees of the 'cause of the Son'. Consequently the ecclesiastical hierarchy appears to be more strongly committed existentially to the Son.

With Otto of Freising, the most important historiographer of the Middle Ages, there appears for the first time the epochal dream that the Kingdom of God might actually be realized in the course of history. His fellow-Cistercian, Joachim of Flora, took up this idea about 1150, dividing world-history into three successive 'Kingdoms of God'. The Old Testament was seen as the Kingdom of the Father, the thousand years of the propagation of the New Testament message as that of the Son; the Kingdom of the Holy Spirit was to follow, a Kingdom of uncontrolled contemplation, of praise of God and the fulness of truth. Here we find the definitive expression of the idea of history as an irreversibly progressive truth-event. The existential bond with the Holy Spirit is predominant for the upholders of this 'third Kingdom'.

The advent of 'institutional lag' is seen in the fact that Church and society did not support the concern of what might be called the 'pneumatic Left' but suppressed that movement. Since the Kingdom of the

Spirit in contemporary awareness was thus postponed to the completely unforeseeable future, the Church succumbed to the illusion of the finality of its structures. The solid self-sufficiency and legalism now emerging were to contribute to the unleashing of the Reformation. The concern of the 'pneumatic Left' was subsequently taken up in heretical quarters, by marginal groups in Christendom, and finally by the splinter-groups of the Reformation. The idea of the Kingdom of God remained active in the form of a longing for a pure community of the Spirit and involved the aspiration to freedom from authoritarian hetero-determination, to equality and to fraternal love of all men. It became the 'prototype of all world-historical Utopias',[3] the driving force which led to the enunciation of the rights of man and in German idealism inspired the 'Revolution of the Spirit'.

### THE HISTORY OF FREEDOM IN MODERN TIMES

Following Pannenberg's lead,[4] I shall attempt briefly to substantiate the thesis that, after the increasing individualization of late medieval times, the above-mentioned Christian ideas arising from the personal understanding of God again become effective as driving forces of the modern age. In this respect it is a question first of the idea of man's resemblance to God, understood as inviolability of personal dignity and as authority to rule over nature. Secondly it is a question of the idea of man's free subjectivity, which is experienced in the light of the Christ-event as existentially free in its decision of love, is aware of itself in the light of the event of the cross as emancipated from total social control, and sees itself through the event of the Spirit on the basis of a progressive awareness of history as committed to a higher freedom, to greater love and to a more complex formation in truth. The importance of these ideas for the individual and society is perceived in a dialectical process and up to a point they are given expression in a secularized form, independent of actual religion and coming into conflict with traditional religious and political authorities.

The relevance of the idea of resemblance to God to structural formation brought about in man at the dawn of modern times a complete awareness of his sovereignty over a disenchanted Nature and an anthropocentrism in the interpretation of his experience of the world. An 'institutional lag' appeared because the rigid late Scholastic type of education was not broken down in time, with the result that humanistic studies came to prevail against the established system of education and were bound to tend towards a naturalism akin to that of antiquity. Moreover, the political and religious authorities had no interest in the rights of man postulated by leading Spanish neo-Scholastic authors of the sixteenth century: such as the right to life, to physical integrity, to marriage and family, to legal protection, to property, to free combination; and the theory of the origin of the State in a contract made by free citizens.[5]

The introduction of free subjectivity in the form of 'congenital rights' or 'rights of man' into the social consciousness of the West is the work of the 'pneumatic Left', which had a revival in the marginal groups of the Reformation. Luther and Calvin themselves had no doctrine of the rights of man. The Reformation brought about a decisive advance in awareness of freedom, not as a doctrine, but as event and as struggle for existence on the part of the Nonconformist or Free Church groups in England in the seventeenth century and in North America in the seventeenth and eighteenth centuries. The Congregationalists especially supported the demand for a pneumatically inspired and democratically structured individual congregation, independent of the established Church. Since we cannot enter here into closer details,[6] we shall simply point to the fact that the Nonconformist groups claimed freedom of religion and of conscience as 'congenital rights' and—where they had to live together with other religious groups, as for instance in the North American colonies—that their influence led to the declaration of full religious freedom for all, for example, in Providence in 1636 and in the purely Catholic colony of Maryland only a year later.

The idea of the rights of man originated essentially in that democratic 'sphere of life' in North America which the Congregationalist John Wise mainly established in the eighteenth century under the motto 'Democracy is Christ's rule in Church and State', and to which he gave a theoretical foundation with the aid of Samuel Pufendorf, the legal philosopher of the early German Enlightenment. Pufendorf's ideas of natural law are still wholly within the Christian tradition and assume that the norms inscribed in human nature have their ground in God. These arguments, founded theoretically and practically in Christianity, strongly support the declarations by the North American states of the rights of man which were to serve as an example for the 'declaration of the rights of man and of the citizen' of the French Revolution.

The enunciation of the rights of subjective freedom—from the standpoint of the history of ideas—is the result of Christian influences. The 'structural lag' is to be found in the fact that the rights of man, confronted with absolutism and the Enlightenment mentality, were necessarily bound to be conceived in an individualistic sense and thus served as a basis for the individualistic-liberal social structure of the subsequent period. The link between the Catholic Church and human rights was broken in the nineteenth century largely because the formulations of these rights—too much concentrated on the individual—seemed to encourage unrestrained libertinism and the abandonment of duty.

On the continent of Europe in the seventeenth and eighteenth centuries the 'pneumatic Left' was able to develop only outside the political sphere. In the conventicles associated with Jakob Boehme, people sought self-redemption under the motto of 'education'. A pietistic movement known as 'Quiet in the land' (cf. Ps. 35:20) produced the German 'Revolution of the Spirit', a movement which tried to be a philosophy simultaneously of history and of salvation. The movement claimed that the new aeon could be brought about only by a transformation of the human spirit in the Holy Spirit. German Romantic thinkers in particular used the term 'Kingdom of God' to describe this expected aeon.

'The revolutionary desire to realize the Kingdom of God is the elastic point of progressive education and the beginning of modern history', wrote Friedrich Schlegal in 1800. We may venture to assert that all the historically effective intellectual movements from the time of the French Revolution onwards responded to the idea that the 'Kingdom of God' could be realized in this world; the pneumaticocentric image of God, however, becomes a variable factor as the core of this idea of the Kingdom, and can even become completely secularized. According to Kant, man takes into himself by means of his reason the continuous revelation of the Holy Spirit. The subject then exists in the fulness of the Spirit, and thus in freedom. For Hegel, absolute spirit as the personification of God is totally actualized as 'Spirit in the community'. Hegel was the last authoritative thinker to describe Christiantiy without qualification as the condition for the history of freedom. According to him, the free subjectivity on which every State is built is lost without Christianity.

## CONCLUSIONS

In the history of the European mind the personal, and particularly the trinitarian, understanding of God has been an essential—if not the most essential—condition for the possibility of existentially free subjectivity, of the explicitation of the rights of man as rights of subjective freedom, of the productive transformation of nature and society, and of progressive education. No comparable development can be observed in the cultural sphere of other religions. An impersonal divinity suggests an unchangeable world-order, representing the reflection of the eternal in time. A fatalistic or resigned surrender to what remains eternally the same inhibits the productive transformation of society and makes man in a general sense 'unpolitical'. If God is understood as personal, history is seen to be a formative process, a progress towards a human being who is more free, more loving and more cultured: in a word, man's evolution to a higher mental complexity.

*Translated by E. Quinn*

*Notes*

1. For a more detailed substantiation of the usefulness of these hypotheses, see G. Wildmann, 'Das personale Gottesverständnis als Bedingung der Freiheitsgeschichte', in K. Krenn (ed.), *Die wirkliche Wirklichkeit Gottes* (Paderborn, 1974), pp. 15—17.

2. I refer here to the theory of 'cultural lag' as first conceived by W. F. Ogburn; but the expression is used only in a loose sense.

3. A. Mirgeler, *Kritischer Rückblick auf das abendländische Christentum* (Freiburg, 1969), p. 145.

4. H. Blumenberg has put forward the thesis that the history of ideas in modern times does not consist in the dialectic of secularized Christian ideas, but represents a break with the ideas of the past and consequently has its own legitimacy (cf. *Die Legitimität der Neuzeit*, 1966). The modern age—he claims—represents the emancipation of reason in the sense of asserting the human personality against the absolutism of forgiveness or damnation taught by the voluntaristic theology of the late Middle Ages. As opposed to this thesis, Wolfhart Pannenberg rightly maintains that voluntarism defended God's freedom and man's against the closed, cosmic system of constraint upheld by the Aristotelianism of the extreme Left. The modern age, he says, is characterized by man's striving for emancipation from the patronage of religious and political authorities. It is a process of secularization preparing for man's coming of age (cf. *Gottesgedanke und menschliche Freiheit* [Göttingen, 1972], especially pp. 124, 127). Secularization means that Christian themes (ideas, motifs, values) continue to exercise an influence, but lose their religious form, since they are withdrawn from the patronage of the Church or substantiated without direct recourse to God.

5. The experiment in applying the rights of man which lasted for two hundred and fifty years under the Jesuit administration in Paraguay seems to have been a merely tolerated arrangement.

6. 'In Christian times the divine Spirit came into the world and made its home in the individual, who is now completely free, having substantial freedom in himself', G. W. F. Hegel, *Vorlesungen über die Philosophie der Weltgeschichte*, Vol. I, ed. Hoffmeister (Hamburg, 1955), p. 157.

# George Maloney

# Prayer and the 'Personal Divine'

IN all human beings there is an inner urging, an élan, towards union with the Other. Throughout all of human history, the ultimate, transcendent Other has been called God. All finite beings must ultimately fail to satisfy this deep-seated hunger for deeper, more intense interpenetration with God.

Religions and prayer forms have been described and distinguished in various ways. Some have been characterized as religions and prayer forms that stress predominately the transcendent, totally 'Other' as God, the source from whom all other creatures flow. He is transcendent and beyond man, incomprehensible, unpossessable, unchanging, eternal in his perfections, completely holy and independent of all outside forces. He is the fire from which all other sparks come; an abyss of infinity separates him from the created world. Judaism and Islam put particular stress on the transcendent God.

Other religions, especially such far-eastern forms as Hinduism and Zen Buddhism, stress the immanence of the Divine. *Advaita*, nonduality, bridges the gap between man and the transcendent God 'outside' or 'up there', and the mystic, through years of self-discipline and psychic purification, finds that he is one with God and the whole of creation.

Because of God's fulness the *Isha Upanishad* sings of the All-in-All that is so deeply within man, and still outside man, that nowhere can man not discover God: 'Plenitude everywhere; plenitude there; plenitude here. From plenitude comes forth plenitude, and everywhere, one with itself, there remains plenitude'.[1]

Bishop Søderbloom, Friedrich Heiler and M. Conrad Hyers have classified religions and prayer forms as *prophetic* or *mystical*. Prophetic religion stresses the awesomeness and dread that comes over the adorer of a most transcendent God in the *mysterium tremendum* of Rudolf Otto, whereas mystical religion stresses the *mysterium fascinans* or movement of ecstatic union or identity.[2]

## THE SYNTHESIS OF CHRISTIANITY

Christianity above all other religions strives to keep a happy tension between these two currents of a God personalized and abiding beyond man the adorer and a God identified with the enlightened man, the mystic. Christianity seeks through the incarnate Word of God and man in one person to synthesize the two, seemingly opposed emphases. God remains always totally 'other' to man, yet through a progressive mystical union God and man become one through grace. God's indwelling life within man assimilates him into the trinitarian life through love which does not destroy man's subjectivity but differentiates his individuality until he becomes aware of his oneness with God.

In oriental mysticism the *coincidentia oppositorum* between the sacred and the profane is an identity of opposites. The profane reality ceases to move, or disappears, becoming identical with the sacred. There is no longer any opposition between the sacred and the profane once *maya* or delusion from the sense world is transcended in the process of enlightenment called *samadhi* or *satori*.

But Christianity, as Nicholas of Cusa and Bonaventure taught, holds the *coincidentia oppositorum* in a tension that is never destroyed as the two move into greater union. Thomas Altizer has well described the Christian dialectic between the sacred and the profane, between God the uncreated and man and his created world: 'When the sacred and profane are understood as dialectical opposites whose mutual negation culminates in a transition or metamorphosis of each into its respective Other, then it must appear that a Christian and eschatological *coincidentia oppositorum* in this sense is finally a coming together or dialectical union in an original sacred and radical profane. Consequently, a consistently Christian dialectical understanding of the sacred must finally look forward to the resurrection of the profane in a transfigured and thus finally sacred form'.[3]

## THE HOLY OTHER

Christianity has always tried to exist in tension between the polarity of God's transcendence and his immament, indwelling presence within the believer. Man cannot see God or know him as he truly is. God must lift the veil of his hiddenness and speak to us through his prophets, especially through his incarnate Word who most perfectly reveals in word and deed the attributes of the person God. Holy Scripture reveals God's awesome presence as a creative power from whose finger tips all creatures tumble: 'Bless the Lord, O my soul; O Lord, my God, thou art very great! Thou art clothed with honour and majesty, who coverest thyself with light as with a garment, who has stretched out the heavens like a tent' (Ps. 104:1–2).

To meet this transcendent God, a Christian must not advance under his own power but, paradoxically, when he falls back in humility before the holy God, he sees by faith through not seeing with his own ideas. God is not a land to be conquered by man's force, but a Holy Land which the Christian approaches with bare feet, as Moses the burning bush—a symbol of total emptiness of his own power. When the Christian in prayer is ready no longer to have his own preconceived ideas about God, God will reveal himself. Man stands before God as Moses did before the bush. He says nothing—for what can he say before the Ineffable? What thought can he think worthy of him who is the Incomprehensible? In adoration, man offers himself to this devouring Fire to be purified of all that is independent self.

The first element, therefore, that Christian prayer shares with Judaism and Islam and other 'prophetic' religions is that God is a person in communication. He is of supreme freedom, independent utterly from his own creation. But to know this person-God, man must be open to God's Word that is the manner of his communication with man, his creature.

Through God's one Word, all creation is brought forth into existence. Mountains and oceans, birds and beasts, flowers and grains tumble forth in profuse richness from the finger tips of the creating God: 'By the word of the Lord the heavens were made, and all their host by the breath of his mouth. He gathered the waters of the sea as though in a bottle; he puts the deeps in storehouses' (Ps. 33:6).

God pulsates with his silent energies in all the inanimate and animate nature of plants, trees, birds and animals that cry out unceasingly to the noisy pilgrims on the roadside, '. . . in him we live and move and have our being' (Acts 17:28). God has created all things in and through the Word and without this Word nothing that has been created can exist (Jn. 1:2).

Revelation of God in Scripture shows us God as love. To posit an act of love, to create out of love, is to be a knowing and loving being. 'God is love. In this the love of God was made manifest among us, that God sent his only Son into the world, so that we might live through him' (1 Jn. 4:9–10). The love of God is therefore the reason for man's existence. If man is a person whose greatest fulfilment comes through self-surrendering in love to another, this is possible only because 'God is love, and he who abides in love abides in God, and God abides in him' (1 Jn. 4:16).

Man is the overflow of God's fulness. In his utter selflessness because he was All, God's goodness created men, not to receive a needed love from him in return, but in order to pour out of the infinite abundance of his being shared-life-in-love. This mystery, revealed to us by the eternal Word of the Father, assures us that we have been made by God out of love, in love and destined for love by participating in God's own life. This living Word came that we might have God's own life and have it more abundantly (Jn. 10:10).

The whole universe has its meaning, its *logos*, its *raison d'être*, only in and through the divine Logos. Man's full nature is man in whom the Logos lives. Man has been made 'according to the image and likeness' (Gen. 1:26) that is Jesus Christ. The image of God in man consists ultimately in possessing the spiritual faculties of intellect and will as a human person through which instruments man may posit himself as an *I*, dependent on the absolute *I* of God. God creates man not as a totally independent being but precisely as a self-positing being in reference to a prototype. That prototype is the divine Word, the 'image of the invisible God', as St Paul describes Christ (Col. 1:15).

Emil Brunner appropriately describes the personalism involved in this relationship between God the Creator and man the creature: 'God creates man in such a way that in this very creation man is summoned to receive the Word actively, that is, he is called to listen, to understand and to believe. God creates man's being in such a way that man knows that he is determined and conditioned by God and in this fact is truly human. The being of man as an "I" is being from and in the divine "Thou", or, more exactly, from and in the divine Word, whose claim "calls" man's being into existence . . . The characteristic imprint of man, however, only develops on the basis of divine determination, as an answer to a call, by means of a decision. The necessity for decision, an obligation which he can never evade, is the distinguishing feature of man . . . it is the being created by God to stand "over against" Him who can reply to God and who in this answer alone fulfils—or destroys —the purpose of God's creation'.[4]

## GOD DWELLS WITHIN MAN

But precisely because the Christian God is so perfect, completely transcendent and holy without the need to be perfected by any outside agent, he becomes through his own free act of love immanently present to man in a new and most personalistic way: 'If a man loves me, he will keep my word, and my father will love him, and we will come to him and make our home with him' (Jn. 14:23). This is the good news that has to be preached from the house tops. Man is a temple of God who dwells within him (1 Cor. 3:16). Man can never be lonely again once he experiences through the faith of the Holy Spirit that he is a child of God and he can call out 'Abba, Father' (Rom. 8:15, 17; Gal. 4:6) for he is an heir of God through Christ.

The Kingdom of God is within man (Lk. 17:21). Man's end is to contemplate the immanent God living within man and thus learn to adore and to serve him dwelling immanently throughout all of creation. As man becomes more aware of God's presence as not distant and extrinsic to man, he moves into a deep unity where his true self becomes a being in loving relationship to the indwelling God.

The central teaching of Christianity is that God, by grace, is present in the soul of man, but only those who advance in deep prayer begin to live in the conscious awareness of this mystical union with God. It is not a union that destroys identity. Teilhard de Chardin rightly describes the essence of Christian prayer in terms of love: 'Love unites as it differentiates'. The essence of Christian belief and Christian prayer that makes it different from all other religions is that God is not only one in essence but three individuated persons: Father, Son and Holy Spirit. The Father empties himself in kenotic love by pouring the fulness of his being into his Word, his only-begotten Son that is the perfect image (icon) of the Father. He does this through the silent gasp of love that is the Holy Spirit. The Son surrenders himself back to the Father through the same Holy Spirit, the binding love of the Father for the Son and the Son for the Father.

This Trinity of Persons, distinct, yet not separated, lives within the Christian. The Father continues to beget his Son through his Spirit within the Christian. The highest degree of contemplation, as the Greek Fathers, especially Maximos the Confessor, describe it, is *theoria theologica* or true *theology*. God no longer reveals himself through the *logoi* in creatures but the trinitarian life unfolds within the soul of the Christian and is experienced in contemplation. A union of man's humanity with God's divinity takes place similar to the *perichoresis*, the circumincession of the two natures in the hypostatic union, human and divine. This, however, is not the hypostatic union but the union between God, the Trinity, and man the adorer through divine grace, the uncreated energies of the indwelling Trinity, divinizing man into a loved and loving child of God.

God reveals himself now through no concepts derived from man's reason but only through an immediate awareness given to man of God's holy and loving presence. In that awareness by experiential knowledge, man becomes through divinization (*theosis*), through a participation in grace, what Jesus Christ was by nature. God is no longer an object to man. A union now of perfect inner communication and interpenetration takes place. Man enters into God. Although man still exists as a human being, yet he knows now a new mode of existence. Two wills in love are virtually one.

As the Christian in prayer experiences more and more the oneness and the many, the union with the Trinity and himself that calls himself into the unique *I* that he is, called into ever greater being by the *Thou* of God's activating presence of love within man, he is able to contemplate God also immanently involved inside the creative process through His 'uncreated energies'. The world of history is a concern for the loving activity of God. Through the crucified Jesus Christ, his Word, obedient unto death, the death of the cross (Phil. 2:8), God has glorified him by raising him as the new Adam and has inserted him into matter as the leaven that draws all things into the unity planned by the Father from all eternity.

God is present to man and creation in his energies and in a very exciting, new way now through the resurrection. The world is constantly bathed in the grace of the divine energies. All is gift. All is grace. God does not simply create in a deistic fashion and let the world develop 'naturally' by itself. God continues to be involved, manifesting his love through his activating energies. It is the total Trinity in dynamic self-giving outwardly to man. Yet God, through Jesus Christ and his Spirit, calls man into that dynamic action of bringing the world of history into the completed new creation: 'Therefore, if anyone is in Christ, he is a new creation; the old has passed away, behold, the new has come. All this is from God, who through Christ reconciled us to himself and gave us the ministry of reconciliation, that is, in Christ God was reconciling the world to himself, not counting their trespasses against them, and entrusting to us the message of reconciliation. So we are ambassadors for Christ . . .' (2 Cor. 5:17–9).

### IMPERSONALIZED DIVINITY

Many far-eastern religions employ an apophatic language so severely that it seems their devotees deny the very personhood of God. The 'emptiness' or 'void' that is the state the eastern mystic seeks to attain in order to be identified with the Absolute is often not so much a theological statement as it is a psychological description of a mystic well advanced in union with the Absolute. To the Westerner such language implies an environment in which the mystic and God merge into one, leaving no individuation, either in God or in the mystic. If, however, we substitute the false-ego of Jung or the attachment to self of Maximos the Confessor, then perhaps the negative side of such a prayer form says that nothing exists completely isolated from the rest of the universe. All living beings and the non-living environment function together as parts of a whole. Concretely, then, such a mystic moves with compassion from such a oneness with his true Ego to every part of the universe as to a part of himself.

Christianity, through its revelation, especially concretized by the incarnate Word, saves the Christian from projecting a psychological description onto objective reality by declaring the *coincidentia oppositorum*. It declares that we are all interrelated through God's Logos in whom and by whom all are created. While saying we are all one, Christianity not only reveals to us that we are always, even in the greatest union with God and creature with other creatures, uniquely different and distinct from God and all other creatures, but through the Church, Jesus Christ gives us his Spirit who alone makes this paradoxical tension a lived reality.

## LOVE AND HUMILITY

Whatever other religions say about personalized or impersonalized Divinity, it is the life of the individual person who prays and meets that Divinity that shows the world whether he not only believes that God is a person but also that he has truly encountered the Other as person. His life will show that at the heart of being a person is the movement outwards toward other free-positing persons through love and humble service. Jesus Christ taught us that by his fruits a man would be known as Jesus' follower.

A Christian experiences in prayer the fact that God is three Persons in a loving union that divinizes the Christian into that same community of one and many. A fully-realized Christian is a man completely stripped of all sinful attachments so that under the illumination of the Holy Spirit he can contemplate the different *logoi* in the Logos, Jesus Christ. By seeking to live his life according to the Logos, he understands the meaning of a human life. His attitudes differ from non-Christians in regard to war, abortion, poverty, work, marriage, ecology, and so on. Such a Christian rooted in the personage of God, three in one, sees through contemplation the power of Jesus Christ working in the lives not only of Christians but of all human beings, regardless of culture or religion. He becomes a citizen of the whole universe. He breaks through the ghetto-concepts of how Jesus Christ should and must work in his universe to see him in a constant process of evolving the universe into its fulness through the basic goodness in human beings. He begins to see through technology that God is bringing about a cosmic consciousness in the minds of all men throughout the whole world. Psychologically, such Christians no longer live in their own little town or city or nation but are beginning to think as citizens of one gigantic 'global village'.

Such a Christian sees that 'matter is sacred' in the sense of being the point of encounter with a dynamic Trinity that, out of love for mankind and a desire to share its divine life with human beings, is found 'inside' all created beings. God's material world has not been conceived by God to be destroyed but to be transfigured and brought into its fulness in and by Jesus Christ.

God calls us to love, to be unique persons in the experience of his unique love for each of us. We are to spend our eternity growing in the love of God as mirrored in other beings. Heaven is going to be this whole wonderful world transfigured by the presence of God through an ever-increasing degree of consciousness of his personalized presence and love. By our ability to be persons and to go out and love others as unique persons just as God has loved us, we can test whether God has really brought us to a true experience in contemplation of the indwelling Trinity. A contemplative sees himself as a person loved by God very much, and in this grace he discovers himself more centred upon God, more one with God, and yet more one with all other beings. There is no longer fear or a sense of insecurity. He is rooted in the personalized love of God for himself and thus he can go forth and love the world as God loves it and with God's very energetic, personalized love living within him.

We evolve into unique persons by the degree of unselfish love-energy within us. But this is shown by humble service toward others whom we recognize by God's illumination within us as unique persons because of God's unique loving activity in their lives. True love that is God's *agape* within man is shown by the readiness to become a person by forgetting the limitations of self-containment and humbly stretching out to serve the other. Christian prayer is the fulfilment of what Jesus Christ taught us: we must lose our life in order to obtain it. We become more the unique persons that God intended us to be from all eternity when he created us in his Logos, if we let the unique, loving persons of the Trinity within us impel us forth to create the *koinonia*, the Body of Christ, by the power of the Holy Spirit who alone unites as he differentiates.

## Notes

1. The Isha Upanishad, cited by Swami Abhishiktananda, in *Hindu-Christian Meeting Point: Within the Cave of the Heart* (Bandra-Bombay, 1969), p. 65.

2. For a modern interpretation of these categories see M. Conrad Hyers, 'Prophet and Mystic: Toward a Phenomenological Foundation for a World Ecumenicity', in *Cross Currents*, Autumn 1970, pp. 6–7.

3. Thomas J. J. Altizer, 'The Sacred and the Profane: A Dialectical Understanding of Christianity', in *Radical Theology and the Death of God*, Thomas J. J. Altizer and William Hamilton (eds.) (Indianapolis, 1965), p. 146.

4. Emil Brunner, *Man in Revolt* (London, 1953), pp. 97–98.

# PART V

*Bulletin*

Robert Mellert

# Process Theology and
# God's Personal Being

OVER a decade has passed since the 'death-of-God' theology came to
a crest in America. Today scarcely a ripple of interest remains. Most of
its proponents have abandoned religious concerns in favor of secular
ones. Many have simply become Christian or Marxist humanists. A
few have made a Barthian act of faith and returned to orthodoxy.

Other groups of American theologians, however, have continued to
scan the waters, attempting to find some suitable philosophical point at
which to re-anchor the traditional Christian belief in a personal God.
One such group, generally called process theologians, rejects the static,
substance-dominated tradition of Aristotle and Aquinas in favour of
the process metaphysics articulated by the English mathematician-
philosopher, Alfred North Whitehead (1861–1947).

## PROCESS AND RELATEDNESS

Two essential tenets of Whiteheadian metaphysics are process and relatedness, and these imply that time and location are necessary ingredi-
ents of every metaphysical situation. Every actuality, including the
divine actuality, must, at least in some sense, be somewhere at some
point in time. To speak of an actuality without spatial and temporal
thickness is to speak of a pure abstraction. If God is real, therefore, he
too must, in some sense, be temporal and spatial.

The use of process categories to describe the Deity entails the abandonment of the classical notion of divine simplicity. Process theology
locates within the Divinity the very oppositions which generally constitute the distinctions of traditional natural theology, such as time and

eternity, responsiveness and changelessness, the conceptual and the physical.

This is not as radical as it may seem. Every moment, or occasion of human experience is a synthesis of its relevant past brought to actualization in a new way. Whiteheadians call these experiences 'actual occasions', or 'actual entities', and they constitute the fundamental actualities of process philosophy. In each such actuality we find both continuity with the past and the emergence of novelty. The physical data grasped in the experience are integrated with a new conceptuality, resulting in a new actuality. Sometimes the novelty is striking; more generally, reiteration predominates.

The conceptual and the physical, therefore, stand not as distinct, antithetical realities, but as a single di-polar tension in the make-up of an actual entity. God, too, can be conceived as embodying these two poles. Process theologians call them the primordial and consequent natures of God.

## THE PRIMORDIAL AND CONSEQUENT NATURES OF GOD

The primordial nature, which corresponds roughly to the conceptual pole in an occasion of human experience, is in God the realm of pure possibility. Here God's function is to envisage the totality of possibility and to hold it available for concrete process. Considered only in his primordial nature, God is deficient of actuality. This is the completely abstract, eternal side of God, to which time and space are metaphysically inappropriate. Thus, there can be no interaction with particulars. In Whitehead's metaphor, God in his primordiality is 'alone with himself'.

The deficiency of actuality in God's primordial nature is completed by the consequent nature, through which God is intrinsically related to all other reality. This is the physical side of God, in which all past data (for in God every past event is relevant) are everlastingly preserved. This nature is also God's changing, temporal aspect, for to it is systematically added each moment of novelty as it is occasioned in the world. Each spatio-temporal actuality that emerges in the world ultimately contributes itself to this physical side of God, wherein God encompasses all fact. What we do makes a difference to God. Whitehead characterizes God in this physical, temporal nature as 'the fellow sufferer who understands'.

## GOD'S RELATEDNESS

This model of God formulated by process theology results from the more general suppositions of Whiteheadian philosophy. First, in accordance with the metaphysical tenet of relatedness, process theology posits a real relation of God to the world, as well as a real relation of the world to God. Hence, it is as true to say that God needs the world as it is to say that the world needs God. God and the world stand in polar tension, such that no meaning could be discovered for either without the simultaneous reality of the other.

The real relation of the world to God has a strong theological tradition. The converse real relation, implying God's dependence upon the world, is less familiar, and perhaps suggests certain questions about God's existence as a distinct, separate being. This problem emphasizes a fundamental difference between process thought and traditional philosophy. The former does not begin with the hypothesis of individual substances identifying distinct beings. Instead it begins with the real relatedness of reality, finding individuality at the confluence of a given set of relations. It denies the notion of an underlying substance or being as the basis of individuality. The becoming of a new actuality in space and time is occasioned by an incorporation of past data and new ideals at a particular locus. And, once achieved, this actual occasion surrenders itself as a datum for new emergence. In Whitehead's famous metaphysical summation of process, 'The many become one and are increased by one'.

God is no exception to the metaphysical principle of relatedness. His individuality is not explicable apart from his relation to the world. God is different from other actualities in that he is occasioned everlastingly: that is, he is constantly incorporating into himself the stream of becomings of the rest of reality. But apart from his real relatedness to that reality, there could be no God, because for process philosophers there is no underlying substance to individuate God or any other entity. Realities are constituted by their relatedness; they are not simply modified by that relatedness. God acquires his actuality from the world. The world's contribution of itself to God gives him his physical nature, individuates him, and saves him from pure abstraction. Hence, it gives God a place in reality, fulfilling one of the conditions for being real.

### GOD'S TEMPORALITY

Second, following the principle of process in Whiteheadian philosophy, process theology posits temporality in God, which is the other condition for reality. The real relatedness between God and the world requires a temporal medium for its operation. God changes. The mutability of God is required by the divine activity of assuming and preserving immortally all past data and making them available for the future. This function is God's consequent, or physical nature, whereby he is always acquiring new facts and constantly being fulfilled.

Again, some questions arise. How is temporality reconciled with the notion of divine perfection? For change seems to imply imperfection, either before or after its occurrence. Can a changing God be all perfect? Charles Hartshorne, a student of Whitehead and an eminent process philosopher himself, resolves the problem by distinguishing between absolute and relative perfection. The latter implies unsurpassability by any except the entity itself. In all cases where temporality makes absolute perfection impossible, we can posit the relative perfection of God: that is, his perfection is such that it is necessarily more perfect than any other actuality and yet is surpassable by God himself at some later stage of process. God is thus not limited to a static, unchanging existence, metaphysically different from the world of flux. He, too, changes, as the world changes.

### THE PROCESS MODEL OF GOD

Clearly, the philosophical suppositions of process thought create a totally new image of God. It is neither the image of traditional theology, which maintains that God is totally independent of and only rationally related to the rest of reality, nor is it the image of pantheism, which holds that God is identical with the rest of reality. The process model of God has, perhaps, been more accurately described as pan*en*theism: that is, the world is in God, but God and the world are distinct realities.

Panentheism is based upon a real distinction between God and the world and upon a mutual, real relation between God and the world. On the one hand, the entity of God is distinct from the world because he embodies the totality of possibility, including the infinite possibilities that are incompatible with the *de facto* structure of existing cosmic reality. God is also unique in that he incorporates into himself all past data. On the other hand, the interrelation of God and the world is essential to each of them, as we have already seen in discussing the doctrine of relatedness. Process theology's model of God agrees with traditional theism and differs from pantheism in maintaining God's individuality; it agrees with pantheism and differs with traditional theism in maintaining mutual and real interrelation. I am suggesting, therefore, that the process model of God can be said to have personal characteristics without encountering the difficulties that plague the traditional approach.

The process model of God can be called personalistic because, by positing temporality and relatedness in God, it provides Christian belief with a metaphysical foundation for genuine communication between God and the world. God can become more religiously available to mankind, and the traditional gulf between the God of the philosopher and the believer's God can be bridged.

## A SERIES OF ACTUAL ENTITIES OR A SINGLE, ENDURING ACTUALITY?

Process theologians argue among themselves whether the ontological structure of God is better understood as a series of actual entities or as a single, enduring actuality. The advantage of the former position is that its description of God is the same ontologically as its description of a human person: both consist of a spatio-temporal series of actual entities which constitute the reality we call 'person'. Hartshorne, opting for this approach, explains that the divine person contains the absolute, not the other way around. The series of entities which identifies the person of God also identifies the absolute in the Divinity.

My own preference, however, is the latter, in which God's ontological structure as a single, enduring entity is different from that of a human person. For belief in a personal God requires that God function interpersonally: that is, the possibilities of human communication with God and of God's power to effect change. It does not seem necessary that God should be described according to the same ontological structure used to describe a human person, for us to relate to his personalistic characteristics.

## PERSONALISTIC LANGUAGE

Consequently, the second option, as well as the first, allows the theologian to use personalistic language when speaking about the Divinity. Such language is appropriate beyond the anthropomorphic sense because personalistic characteristics are appropriate to a Divinity whose structure, as spatio-temporal and interrelated with the world, thereby includes the possibility of mutual communication and influence. When we say, for example, that God reveals himself, or that he hears prayers, we are not speaking about a relation to a supreme, transcendent, or metaphysically distinct being, but about a concrete relation in which God and the world are integral. God reveals himself out of the fund of past data and in the possibilities available for the future. Our petitions to him are answered in the fuller understanding of his reality and in the relevant possibilities for our own. This communication is neither shrouded in mystery nor a mere psychological uplifting. It is a genuine communication with a Deity who is with us in space and time.

Divine revelation and God's response to prayer are based upon the power of God to communicate back to the world. Divine power is not the power to coerce, but to persuade. God lures the world towards the ideal, the novel, the interesting. As Whitehead put it: 'The power of God is the worship he inspires'.

A personal God is one who communicates and has power. If the Christian belief in a personal God is truly the reflection of humanity's striving to communicate with the Divinity and to be on the side of his power, then I believe that process theology can be a most useful instrument of support for that belief.

## Bibliography

John B. Cobb, *A Christian Natural Theology* (Philadelphia, 1965).
Charles Hartshorne, *The Divine Relativity* (New Haven, 1948).
Robert B. Mellert, *What Is Process Theology?* (New York, 1975).
Alfred North Whitehead, *Process and Reality* (New York, 1929).
———, *Religion in the Making* (Cleveland, 1960).

# Contributors

RANIERO CANTALAMESSA, O.F.M., Cap., was born in Ascoli, Italy, in 1934. He is Professor and Director of the Department of Religious Science at the Catholic University of Milan. Among his publications are *La cristologia di Tertulliano* (Fribourg, 1962) and *Il cristienesimo e i valori terreni. Sessualità, impegno politico e cultura* (Milan, 1976).

FRANS MAAS, O.C.D., was born in Turnhout, Belgium, in 1946. He is at present a lecturer in fundamental theology at the Catholic Theological University in Amsterdam. He has published a number of articles and a selection, with introduction, of extracts from the works of Meister Eckhart: *Van God als van Niemand, Preken van Eckhart* (Haarlem, 1975).

GEORGE MALONEY, S.J., was born in Green Bay, Wisconsin. He is a member of the Pope John XXIII Centre for Eastern Studies and teaches oriental theology and spirituality at Fordham University. He was founder-editor of *Diakonia*. His latest books are *Inward Stillness, Mary, the Womb of God* and *A History of Orthodox Theology Since 1453*.

ROBERT MELLERT teaches philosophy at Brookdale College, Lincroft, New Jersey, U.S.A. His most recent publication is *What is Process Theology?*. He is working on a book on process ethics.

PETER NEMESHEGYI, S.J., was born in Budapest in 1923. Since 1956 he has taught fundamental and dogmatic theology at Sophia University, Tokyo. Among his many works (including some in Hungarian and Japanese) is *Le paternité de Dieu chez Origène* (Paris, 1960).

JAN PETERS, O.C.D., was born in Elsloo, the Netherlands, in 1921. He has published a number of works on prayer. He has translated into

Dutch and introduced the works of St John of the Cross as *Mystieke werken van Sint-Jan van het Kruis* (Ghent, 1975).

PIET SCHOONENBERG, S.J., was born in Amsterdam in 1911. He is Professor of Dogmatic Theology at the University of Nijmegen. He is the author of many leading theological works.

MANFRED VOGEL was born in Israel in 1930. He is Professor of Jewish Thought in the Department of History and Literature of Religions, at Northwestern University, Evanston, Illinois, U.S.A. He has written many articles and books and has translated and introduced Feuerbach's *Principles of the Philosophy of the Future* (Indianapolis and New York, 1966).

HERBERT VORGRIMLER was born in Freiburg-im-Breisgau, Germany, in 1929. He is Professor of Dogmatics and the History of Dogma in the Faculty of Catholic Theology in the University of Münster. His most recent publication is *Eschatologie* (1977).

FALK WAGNER was born in Vienna in 1939. He studied theology, sociology and philosophy in Mainz and Frankfurt and under Wolfhart Pannenberg in Munich. Among his publications are *Über die Legitimität der Mission* (Munich, 1968) and *Schleiermacher's Dialektik* (Gütersloh, 1974).

GEORG WILDMANN was born in Yugoslavia in 1929. He is Professor of Religion and Philosophy at a College of Education in Linz. Among his publications is *Personalismus, Solidarismus und Gesellschaft. Der ethische und ontologische Grundcharakter der Gesellschaftslehre der Kirche* (Vienna, 1961).